SEDC

GUIDE 2025

A Local Manual Including Hiking Trails, Historic sites, Adventures, Tips and more

Jacalyn E. Williams

2

All Rights Reserved!

No part of this book may be reproduced, stored in a retrieval system, or transmitted in any form or by any means, electronic, mechanical, photocopying, recording, or sotherwise, without the prior written permission of the copyright owner. Copyright 2024, Jacalyn E. Williams.

DISCLAIMER

This Travel Guide is provided for informational purposes only. Although every effort is made to ensure the accuracy and reliability of the information, the publisher does not guarantee the completeness, accuracy, or reliability of the guide.

All content is provided "as is," and reliance on the information in this guide is strictly at your own risk. The publisher will not be liable for any losses or damages arising from the use of this guide, including, but not limited to, indirect or consequential loss or damage, or any loss or damage whatsoever resulting from loss of data or profits arising out of, or in connection with, the use of this guide.

Information in this guide may change, and it is recommended to confirm details with official sources and local authorities before making travel arrangements. This guide is designed to assist you in discovering and exploring breathtaking landscapes, vibrant cultures, and unique experiences.

TABLE OF CONTENT

Introduction to Sedona: the Land of Red Rocks. 9
Understanding Sedona 13
    History and Culture of Sedona 13
    Geography and Climate 14
    Travel Tips 15
Planning Your Sedona Trip: A Comprehensive Guide 18
    Best time to visit Sedona 18
    Visa and Travel Information 19
    Travel Essentials 20
    Budgeting for Your Trip 21
Navigating Sedona: A Comprehensive Travel Guide 23
    Arriving at Sedona. 23
    Transportation Options in Sedona. 24
    Transportation Tips 25
Sedona's Accommodations: From Luxurious Resorts to Unique Local Stays. 28
    Luxury resorts 28
    Mid-range Hotels 30
    Budget Stays. 31
    Unique Local Accommodations 32
Savoring Sedona: A Culinary Journey Through Red Rock Country. 34
    Local delicacies 34
    Top Restaurants. 35
    Street Food and Snack Stops. 36
    Vegan and vegetarian options. 37

Preparing for Your Hike: The Sedona Way..39
    Essential Gear and Supplies 39
    Understanding Sedona Weather Patterns 41
    Safety Tips and Trail Etiquette..42
    Permit Requirements and Regulations 42
Discover Sedona: Easy Trails for Every Beginner 44
Sedona's Scenic Challenge: Moderate Trails for Experienced Hikers. ...48
Sedona's Ultimate Challenge: Trails for Adventure Seekers...................52
Cathedral Rock: A Spiritual Journey Through Sedona's Red Rocks. 56
Bell Rock Pathway: Exploring Iconic Views in Sedona's Red Rock Wonderland 61
Soldier Pass Trail: Caves, Arches, and Pools in Sedona's Red Rocks 65
Devil's Bridge: A Magnificent Journey Through Sedona's Iconic Landscape. 70
Boynton Canyon: Exploring Energy Vortexes and Ancient Echoes........75
Explore Sedona: Special Interest Hiking Adventures..............................79
    Family-Friendly Hikes 79
    Pet-friendly trails 80
    Best Sunrise and Sunset Spots 81
    The Geological Wonders of Sedona 82
Sedona's Seasonal Hiking Guide: Accepting Nature's Rhythms.............84
    Spring: Wildflowers and Cacti Bloom 84
    Summer: Monsoons and Night Hikes 86
    Autumn: Colors and Cooler Trails..87
    Winter: Snow-capped Red Rocks..88
Sedona: An Exploration of History, Culture, and Nature 90
    History of Hiking in Sedona 90
    The Evolution of Hiking Trails in the Modern Period 92

Native American Heritage Sites..93
Ceremonial Sites and Energy Vortexes 94
Historic Sites Along the Trails of Sedona 100
Outdoor Adventures in Sedona: Exciting Events for Nature Lovers....105
Hiking and Trail Exploration 105
Mountain Bike Adventures 106
Rock climbing and canyoneering 107
Water Activities...108
Camping and stargazing..109
Upcoming events for outdoor enthusiasts. 109
Sedona Hike: A Photographer's Paradise. 113
Photographic Hotspots 113
Tips for capturing the perfect sunset. 115
Shopping In Sedona: A Treasure Trove of Unique Finds and Local Crafts.
....119
Best Shopping Districts in Sedona....................................119
Local Handicrafts and Souvenirs 121
Shopping Tips 122
Practical Travel Information for Sedona: Essentials for A Safe And Enjoyable Trip...124
Health and Medical Services 124
Safety Tips 126
Common Local Customs and Etiquette 127
Conclusion: Maximizing Your Sedona Experience. 130
Last-Minute Travel Tips...130
How to make the most of your visit 132
Appendix...134
Useful Apps...134

7

Travel Checklist 134
Emergency Contacts 135
Frequently Asked Questions 135
Suggested Travel Itineraries 137

Introduction to Sedona: The Land of Red Rocks.

Sedona, Arizona, is considered one of the most scenic destinations in the United States, and its allure draws explorers, spiritual seekers, and nature lovers alike. Its unique red rock landscapes are a visual feast and a spiritual retreat, offering limitless opportunities for exploration and introspection.

The red rocks of Sedona are more than just breathtaking natural creations. These sandstone monoliths, set against pure blue skies, offer a visual spectacle that changes with the sun, shining brightly at daybreak and dusk. Each rock formation, from Bell Rock to Cathedral Rock, presents a distinct story of geological history spanning millions of years. Sedona's scenery is a dynamic canvas, with lush vegetation after summer rains and vivid wildflowers in the spring, providing layers of contrast to the iron-rich rocks.

Sedona is frequently called a spiritual paradise because of its numerous energy vortexes, which many believe to be energy centers conducive to healing, meditation, and self-discovery. Sedona's vortexes attract those seeking to improve their spiritual practice or simply find a moment of serenity in the frenetic pace of modern life. Hiking in Sedona provides more than just physical fitness; it also allows you to discover the spiritual landscape that Native American tribes have revered for ages.

With almost 300 miles of trails, Sedona is a hiker's dream. Trails range from pleasant hikes for families to challenging treks for experienced hikers seeking a challenge. Each route provides a distinct view of Sedona's enormous scenery. The trails' accessibility assures that anyone, regardless of hiking ability, may enjoy the area's rough beauty.

Each season in Sedona puts the city in a unique light. The moderate winters are ideal for anyone wishing to escape the harsh cold of the north, with temperate days and the occasional thin dusting of snow that highlights the red rocks against the pure white. Spring is a renewal period for the flora and the emergence of new wildlife, making it excellent for photographers and environment lovers. Summer in Sedona can be hot, but the higher elevation and cool monsoon showers in the afternoon make it ideal for early-morning treks. Autumn cloaks the Valley in colder temperatures and brings a flood of golden hues, creating a stunning backdrop for late-year walks.

Sedona's rich cultural tapestry is weaved from its Native American heritage, pioneer past, and reputation as an artist colony. The preserved ruins and the stories local guides and historians provide demonstrate the town's appreciation for its legacy. Sedona's artistic community thrives thanks to galleries, festivals, and a culture celebrating creativity. This combination of environment and culture provides a well-rounded vacation that can satisfy both the need for adventure and artistic inspiration.

Recognizing the fragile beauty of its surroundings, Sedona is dedicated to conservation efforts. The trails are well-kept, and there are several opportunities for visitors to learn about the necessity of protecting this unspoiled environment. Local businesses rely on an eco-friendly mentality, providing anything from sustainable housing to tours that protect wildlife habitats.

Sedona promises a journey that is both enriching and stunning. Whether hiking the broad trails at dawn, investigating the spiritual importance of its landscapes, or enjoying the warm friendliness of its residents, Sedona provides an opportunity to reconnect with nature and get a new perspective. The red rocks of Sedona are more than just a destination; they offer a gateway to new adventures, new insights, and unforgettable encounters. Welcome to Sedona; let your trip begin.

Understanding Sedona

History and Culture of Sedona

Nestled amidst Arizona's towering red rock formations, Sedona has a history as vivid as its famous sandstone cliffs. Before becoming a destination for artists, spiritual seekers, and nature lovers, Sedona was home to Native American tribes like the Sinagua, Yavapai, and Apache. The rich cultural tapestry of these tribes is woven into the very fabric of the area, as seen by the rock art, cliff dwellings, and cultural items found throughout the landscape.

Pioneers moved to the area in the late nineteenth and early twentieth century, enticed by the promise of mineral wealth and the land's beauty. Sedona's name derives from Sedona Miller Schnebly, the wife of the city's first postmaster, known for her friendliness and vivacious personality. As the twentieth century proceeded, Sedona became known as a haven for artists and filmmakers lured to its stunning scenery and tranquil surroundings. This artistic legacy lives on today, with various galleries, festivals, and seminars dedicated to promoting and nurturing creative creativity.

Geography and Climate

Sedona is located at the mouth of Oak Creek Canyon and is known for its stunning red rock formations, including Bell Rock, Cathedral Rock, and Courthouse Butte. These geological wonders are mostly red sandstone, formed by natural forces over millions of years. The city is also surrounded by 1.8 million acres of National Forest, providing several hiking, biking, and camping options.

Sedona's warm and semi-arid climate makes it an ideal year-round getaway. Summers are warm but not extremely hot because the height is around 4,500 feet above sea level, which relieves the strong heat across Arizona. Winters are chilly, and snow occasionally falls, providing a striking contrast to the red cliffs. Spring and autumn are especially nice, with temperate temperatures and perfect weather for outdoor activities.

Travel Tips

When planning a trip to Sedona, consider the time of year. Spring and October provide the finest weather, avoiding the summer heat and the peak tourist season. These seasons also allow you to witness the landscape evolve, with wildflowers in the spring and blazing golden foliage in the fall.

Getting Around: Renting a car is strongly suggested because public transportation is limited, and many trailheads and attractions are dispersed. Sedona also has various biking routes; hiring a bike is a fun way to explore the area.

Accommodation: Sedona offers a variety of lodging options, including magnificent resorts, quaint bed and breakfasts, campsites, and eco-friendly retreats. Booking in advance is recommended, especially during busy seasons or when local festivities are held.

Respect the Environment: The Sedona community is strongly committed to environmental preservation. Visitors are advised to follow the 'Leave No Trace' guidelines when hiking and exploring. This includes removing all litter, remaining on approved trails, and not disturbing wildlife.

Explore Beyond the Beaten Path: While well-known attractions like Bell Rock and Cathedral Rock are must-sees, Sedona has hidden jewels like secret canyon trails and quiet waterfalls. Local tour guides can provide insights into less-traveled regions that might be overlooked.

Experience Local Culture: Take the time to discover Sedona's cultural offerings. Visit the Tlaquepaque Arts & Crafts Village's art galleries, take in a concert at the Sedona Arts Center, and don't miss the Palatki Heritage Site, where you can learn about local Native American history.

Mind the Vortexes: For those interested in Sedona's spiritual side, consider visiting its famous vortex locations, which are believed to be swirling energy centers conducive to healing and meditation. Whether or not you believe in the vortexes, these sites provide breathtaking views and a moment of tranquility.

Sedona offers a unique combination of adventure, leisure, and cultural enrichment. Sedona's breathtaking natural surroundings, rich history, and active local scene make a tour as diverse and exciting as the landscape.

Planning Your Sedona Trip: A Comprehensive Guide

Welcome to the important resource for arranging your trip to Sedona, Arizona. Sedona, known for its stunning red rock formations and bustling art scene, provides visitors with diverse experiences. Whether looking for outdoor adventures, spiritual development, or a calm escape into nature, carefully organizing your vacation will ensure an unforgettable experience. Let's go into when to visit, travel logistics, crucial packing recommendations, and budgeting for your vacation.

Best time to visit Sedona

Your weather choices and crowd levels determine the best time to visit Sedona. The town's high desert environment provides several seasons, each with its appeal.

Spring (March through May): is undoubtedly the finest time to visit Sedona. The weather is pleasant, with temperatures ranging from the mid-60s to the low 80s (Fahrenheit), and the scenery is colorful with blossoming wildflowers. Spring also provides ideal hiking conditions before the summer heat comes in.

Fall (September to November): Like spring, fall offers pleasant temperatures and the extra spectacle of changing foliage, which paints the canyons in gold and amber. Visitor traffic is typically lighter than in the spring, making popular locations more pleasurable.

Summer (June to August): Sedona's summers are warm, with temperatures frequently reaching the 90s. However, higher elevation means cooler evenings, making early morning and late evening the best periods for outdoor activity. Be aware of the monsoon season in late summer, which might bring unexpected thunderstorms.

Winter (December to February): While the coldest season, with occasional snowfall, Sedona's winter is often moderate and peaceful, making it excellent for visitors seeking seclusion and magnificent snowy red rock landscapes. It's also an excellent time to photograph and appreciate the town's charming amenities without the crowds.

Visa and Travel Information

International tourists must meet strict visa criteria before visiting the United States, which vary based on their country of origin. Most travelers must apply for a B-2 Tourist Visa unless they qualify for the Visa Waiver Program (VWP), which permits visitors from selected countries to enter the United States for 90 days without a visa. Make sure you check the most recent standards for the United States. Visit the Department of State's website or contact the nearest U.S. Embassy or consulate.

Upon arrival, getting travel insurance that covers medical bills, loss, and theft is strongly advised, as healthcare costs in the United States can be enormous without proper coverage.

Travel Essentials

Packing for Sedona involves careful consideration of the season and your planned activities. Here are some crucial items for your packing list:

Clothing: Layering is essential. Pack breathable, moisture-wicking textiles for hiking and thermal layers for cooler evenings. Bring sturdy hiking boots, caps, sunglasses, and sunscreen to protect yourself from the sun.

Navigation Tools: While digital maps are convenient, having a physical map or a GPS gadget can be useful, especially in isolated locations with poor phone coverage.

Hydration and Snacks: Always bring lots of water, as the arid climate can quickly dehydrate you. Long hikes benefit greatly from energy-boosting snacks such as nuts or granola bars.

Photography Equipment: Sedona's beautiful vistas are a photographer's dream, so pack your camera and any essential gear, such as lenses, tripods, and extra batteries.

Budgeting for Your Trip

Your travel style, preferred accommodations, food choices, and planned activities will determine your Sedona vacation budget. Here are some tips for managing your finances:

Accommodation: options range from low-cost motels and campers to luxury resorts and vacation apartments. Booking in advance can help you get better rates, especially during peak seasons.

Dining: Sedona offers a variety of dining alternatives, from informal cafés to upmarket restaurants. If your hotel has a kitchen, you might save money by making some meals.

Activities: Many of Sedona's natural features are free to view, although specialist trips, such as jeep tours, guided hikes, or spiritual experiences, may cost more. Look for package deals or group savings, if available.

Transportation: Renting a car is typically the most convenient way to see Sedona and its surroundings. Compare rental prices and book in advance to get the best offers. Alternatively, use local shuttle services to go around town.

Planning your vacation to Sedona using these suggestions can help you make the most of your time there, whether exploring the magnificent outdoors, delving into the spiritual vortexes, or enjoying the local culture and art scene. With the proper preparation, your Sedona vacation will be enriching and exciting, giving you moments you'll remember for a lifetime.

Navigating Sedona: A Comprehensive Travel Guide

Sedona, with its stunning red rocks and bustling art scene, is more than simply a location; it's an experience that begins as soon as you arrange your visit. Getting to and around Sedona can be as much of an experience as the town's famous hiking and spiritual investigation. Whether you arrive by plane, road, or rail, and whether you like to explore by car, bike, or public transportation, knowing your options will help you make the most of your vacation. Here's everything you should know about getting to and around Sedona.

Arriving at Sedona.

Most visitors to Sedona will fly into Phoenix Sky Harbor International Airport (PHX), roughly two hours south of Sedona by automobile. This major airport serves a wide range of domestic and international flights, making it a handy starting point for your Sedona journey.

From Phoenix to Sedona: Once you arrive, the easiest method to travel to Sedona is to rent a car and drive. The route leads you north on I-17, a picturesque freeway that snakes through the desert before entering the colder climates of Northern Arizona. Car rental services are widely available at the airport, with a wide selection of automobiles to suit all budgets and preferences.

Alternative Airports: Flagstaff Pulliam Airport (FLG) is a smaller regional airport 45 minutes from Sedona. However, flight alternatives here are more limited and sometimes more expensive.

Shuttle Services: If you don't want to drive, various shuttle services run between Phoenix and Sedona. These services provide the convenience of many departures daily and a comfortable journey directly to your Sedona accommodations.

Transportation Options in Sedona.

Once you arrive, there are various transportation alternatives to assist you tour the area:

Renting a car is the most flexible alternative. Sedona and its neighboring attractions, such as the Verde Valley wine region and the ghost town of Jerome, are spread out, and having your vehicle allows you to visit them on your own time.

Bus: The Sedona RoadRunner offers public transportation in Sedona and the surrounding areas, including routes to popular destinations such as Oak Creek Canyon and the Village of Oak Creek. This service is reasonably priced and suitable for individuals seeking to lessen their environmental impact.

Biking: Sedona is extremely bike-friendly, with various routes and lanes around the town. Bike rentals, including high-performance mountain bikes and comfortable cruisers for visiting the town, are provided.

Taxis and rideshare services: such as Uber and Lyft, are available in Sedona, providing handy transportation choices for people without a car. They are especially beneficial in the evenings after long trekking or when you intend to sample some of Sedona's local wines.

Transportation Tips

To make the most of your time in Sedona, consider these suggestions:

Book in Advance: If you're going during high tourist seasons (spring and fall), arrange your car rental or shuttle for the best rates and availability.

Plan Your Route: While Sedona isn't huge, its meandering roads and stunning vistas might make travel times longer than planned. Plan your travels, especially if you have reservations or tours scheduled.

Parking: On weekends, parking might be limited in popular areas such as Uptown Sedona and trailheads. Arrive early to obtain a spot and follow parking restrictions to prevent citations.

Stay Informed: Check local conditions before leaving, especially if you intend to go to more distant places. Seasonal weather can impact road conditions; therefore, planning is always a good idea.

Embrace the Scenery: One of the highlights of Sedona is the drive itself, particularly roads such as the Red Rock Scenic Byway (SR 179) and Oak Creek Canyon (SR 89A). Allow time to safely pull over at designated viewpoints to soak in the scenery—these drives are regarded as some of the most beautiful in America.

Arriving and visiting Sedona provides a balance of ease and adventure. From the moment you land or hit the road, every route delivers stunning sights and the thrill of discovery. With proper planning and knowledge of your transportation options, you'll be well on your way to seeing the best Sedona offers. Enjoy the journey as much as the destination, and allow Sedona's scenery and energy to revive you.

Sedona's Accommodations: From Luxurious Resorts to Unique Local Stays.

Sedona, a jewel tucked among Arizona's red-hued rocks, offers magnificent scenery and a choice of lodging alternatives to complement your vacation. Sedona provides something for everyone, whether you want the indulgence of a luxury resort, the comfort of a mid-range hotel, the affordability of budget stays, or the distinct charm of local accommodations. This detailed guide will show you the best locations to stay in Sedona, ensuring your trip is as memorable as the scenery.

Luxury resorts

Sedona's premium resorts provide world-class services, magnificent amenities, and breathtaking views of the Red Rocks. These resorts are more than just places to stay; they are destinations in their own right.

Enchantment Resort: Enchantment Resort, located in Boynton Canyon, mixes luxury with natural quiet. The resort offers spacious casita-style suites with private patios that overlook the canyon. Guests can relax at the Mii amo spa, dine at a restaurant, or participate in special activities like guided hikes, yoga, and tennis.

L'Auberge de Sedona: Located on the banks of Oak Creek, L'Auberge de Sedona combines rustic charm with luxury. The resort has a range of bungalows, each nicely outfitted with outdoor cedar showers and individual balconies. The L'Apothecary Spa offers personalized spa treatments, while the L'Auberge Restaurant on Oak Creek is one of Sedona's top dining destinations, with cuisine including locally produced products.

Sedona Rouge Hotel & Spa: This sophisticated resort is distinguished by its Mediterranean architecture and brilliant red rock backdrop. The Sedona Rouge features opulent rooms and suites, a full-service spa, and an outdoor pool with breathtaking views. The hotel's Reds Sedona Grill restaurant delivers contemporary American cuisine focusing on comfort and quality.

Mid-range Hotels

Mid-range hotels in Sedona offer comfortable accommodations with various amenities, making them ideal for tourists seeking a balance of comfort and value.

Arabella Hotel Sedona: Situated near the heart of Sedona, Arabella Hotel Sedona provides easy access to the area's well-known vortex sites and hiking trails. With two outdoor pools, a hot tub, and a trailhead on the property, guests may enjoy both rest and adventure.

Sedona Summit Resort by Diamond Resorts: Located on the city's western edge, this resort offers spacious suites with kitchenettes, perfect for families or extended visits. The resort has many outdoor pools and hot tubs, making it an excellent location for visiting adjacent Red Rock State Park.

Best Western Plus Arroyo Roble Hotel & Creekside Villas: With breathtaking views of the red rocks, this hotel offers spacious rooms, indoor and outdoor pools, a fitness center, and convenient access to Uptown Sedona's shops and restaurants.

Budget Stays.

For the budget-conscious traveler, Sedona has various cheap options that do not sacrifice convenience or comfort.

GreenTree Inn Sedona: Located on the outskirts of Sedona, GreenTree Inn provides clean, comfortable accommodations at an affordable price. It offers an outdoor pool, complimentary breakfast, and free Wi-Fi, making it a good deal for budget travelers.

Sedona Village Resort: Located in the Village of Oak Creek, just a short drive from Sedona, this resort is ideal for people who prefer a quieter environment. The accommodations are simple but well-maintained, providing a relaxing escape without breaking the bank.

Sugar Loaf Lodge: This no-frills motel is recognized for its courteous staff and spotless accommodations. With an outdoor pool and a convenient position near hiking trails, it's an excellent alternative for nature enthusiasts wishing to save money on lodging.

Unique Local Accommodations

Sedona offers a variety of local hotels that reflect the area's artistic ethos and connection to nature, making for a unique visit.

Sky Ranch Lodge: Sky Ranch Lodge, located above Airport Mesa, has breathtaking panoramic views of Sedona's red rocks. The lodge has rustic accommodations and a garden setting that is especially picturesque at sunset.

El Portal Sedona Hotel: This boutique hotel has 12 individually created guest suites that reflect the characteristics of the Southwest. El Portal, located near the Tlaquepaque Arts & Crafts Village, offers a magnificent yet personal environment with pet-friendly rooms and a private patio.

The Butterfly Garden Inn: Located in Oak Creek Canyon, this beautiful inn features tiny cottages surrounded by lush gardens and towering pine trees. It's ideal for individuals seeking seclusion and a close touch with nature.

Sedona's varied choice of hotels guarantees that every visitor may find the ideal place to relax after exploring. Whether you choose the lavish comforts of a luxury resort, the dependable quality of a mid-range hotel, the affordability of a budget stay, or the distinct charm of local lodging, your time in Sedona will be enhanced by the warm hospitality and breathtaking natural beauty that these lodgings provide. Each choice offers a unique viewpoint on this wonderful region, allowing you to plan a stay suited to your specific style and tastes.

Savoring Sedona: A Culinary Journey Through Red Rock Country.

Nestled amidst Arizona's towering red rock formations, Sedona is more than just a visual feast; it's also a culinary delight. The city's food scene is as lively and colorful as the surrounding landscapes, with varied flavors to suit every palate. Sedona is a culinary destination worth discovering, with local delicacies that embody the spirit of the Southwest, as well as top-tier restaurants, street-side eateries, and good vegan and vegetarian options. Here's how to enjoy the best eating experiences Sedona has to offer.

Local delicacies

Sedona's cuisine is heavily based on Southwest traditions, focusing on dishes made with native ingredients, including maize, beans, squash, and chiles. Here are some local delights that you should not miss.

Navajo Tacos: are a variation of regular tacos, prepared with frybread rather than tortillas. They're a robust blend of Native American and Southwestern cuisine, with ground beef, lettuce, cheese, and tomato on top.

Chile Rellenos: are green chiles packed with cheese, covered in egg batter, and then fried till golden. Typically served with salsa or enchilada sauce, they provide a spicy kick typical of regional cuisine.

Sedona Corn Chowder: is a creamy combination with a foundation of sweet corn, potatoes, and occasionally roasted green chiles, creating a comforting warmth ideal for chilly evenings in the high desert.

Top Restaurants.

Sedona has numerous amazing restaurants serving great meals and breathtaking views of the area's natural splendor.

Mariposa Latin Inspired Grill: This upmarket restaurant focuses on Latin American cuisine, particularly grilled meats and seafood. The environment is equally striking as the meal, with large windows offering panoramic views of Sedona's red cliffs.

Elote Café: popular among locals and visitors alike, delivers Chef Jeff Smedstad's inventive Mexican-inspired meals. The restaurant's hallmark dish, Elote (fire-roasted corn with spicy mayo, lime, and cotija cheese), is a must-try.

Rene in Tlaquepaque: In the quaint Tlaquepaque Arts & Crafts Village, Rene serves a sophisticated menu with French and Mediterranean influences. The atmosphere is romantic, with intimate dining rooms and a charming patio ideal for a memorable night out.

Street Food and Snack Stops.

For casual nibbles, Sedona's street food and snack places are ideal for replenishing during a day of sightseeing.

Oak Creek Espresso: While primarily a coffee business, it also serves fantastic small meals and pastries, making it an excellent choice for breakfast or a mid-afternoon snack.

Farmers Market: Visit the Sedona Farmers Market to experience fresh produce and local delights from various merchants. It's an excellent place to sample gourmet cheeses, handcrafted jams, and freshly baked pastries.

Tlaquepaque Food Truck Court: Conveniently located in the Tlaquepaque Arts & Crafts Village, this food truck court includes a changing assortment of trucks serving tacos, burgers, and sweet desserts.

Vegan and vegetarian options.

Sedona welcomes individuals who follow a plant-based diet, with numerous restaurants serving inventive vegan and vegetarian dishes.

ChocolaTree: A refuge for health-conscious consumers, ChocolaTree is a 100% organic restaurant with gluten-free and vegetarian cuisine. The garden environment enhances the dining experience, making it a tranquil spot for lunch or dinner.

Picazzo's Healthy Italian Kitchen: Known for its gluten-free offerings, Picazzo's also has a diverse vegan menu. The options are many and satisfying, from vegan pizzas and pasta to creative salads.

Local Juicery: For a quick and nutritious dinner, Local Juicery serves cold-pressed juices, smoothies, and a range of vegan bowls and snacks. Their ingredients are locally obtained, which ensures freshness and quality.

Dining in Sedona is a journey in and of itself, reflecting the area's unique cultural tapestry and breathtaking natural surroundings. Whether indulging in a lavish lunch, enjoying the simplicity of street cuisine, or exploring the numerous vegan and vegetarian alternatives, Sedona's culinary culture guarantees to elevate your vacation with flavors as memorable as the sunsets. Each meal provides an opportunity to engage with local culture and cuisine, making your Sedona experience comprehensive and nutritious.

Preparing for Your Hike: The Sedona Way

Hiking in Sedona, with its distinctive red rock scenery and twisting trails, requires preparation and respect for the environment. Whether planning a leisurely walk down the Valley or a rigorous hike up to Cathedral Rock, knowing what to bring, how to prepare for the weather, and comprehending trail etiquette and laws can help you have a safe and enjoyable adventure. Here's all you need to know to prepare for your hiking trip in Sedona.

Essential Gear and Supplies

The appropriate gear might mean the difference between a demanding but gratifying hike and a difficult, uncomfortable one. Here's a list of essentials to pack:

Hiking Boots: Durable, well-fitting hiking boots or shoes are essential. Sedona's surface can be rough and uneven, so good footwear will give traction and support.

Backpack: A comfortable, lightweight backpack is required to transport your goods. Ensure it has enough compartments to store gear and enough space for extended trips.

Water & Hydration Systems: Dehydration poses a big problem in Sedona's desert climate. Carry more water than you think you'll need, usually around one gallon per person each day. Hydration packs and water bottles are ideal.

Clothing: Wear layers. Lightweight, breathable textiles are ideal for the base layer, with a fleece or wool layer providing insulation. Regardless of the season, always take a waterproof jacket in case of unexpected rain.

Navigation Tools: GPS devices, maps, and compasses are useful, especially on less-marked trails or when traveling in isolated places.

First Aid: Basic first aid supplies include bandages, antiseptic, tweezers, and personal prescriptions. A whistle and a mirror for signaling can also come in handy in an emergency.

Sun Protection: Even on cloudy days, you should wear sunglasses, a wide-brimmed hat, and sunscreen to protect yourself from the sun's UV radiation.

Snacks: Energy bars, almonds, dried fruits, and jerky are ideal for rapid sustenance on a trek.

Understanding Sedona Weather Patterns

Sedona's climate is generally mild, although it can pose issues with unexpected shifts that may impair your hiking plans:

Summer (June to August): Expect scorching temperatures that frequently exceed 90°F. To avoid the noon heat, go hiking early or late in the evening. The monsoon season begins in late summer, with afternoon thunderstorms that can produce flash flooding.

Fall (September through November) is one of Sedona's best seasons for hiking. The weather is colder and more consistent, with little rain and pleasant daytime temperatures.

Winter (December to February) brings colder daytime temperatures and the possibility of snowfall. At the same time, lovely snow may make trails treacherous and difficult to navigate.

Spring (March to May) is similar to autumn, with warm weather and increased natural beauty as flowers bloom.

However, spring offers changeable weather, including the possibility of late snowfalls or rain showers.

Safety Tips and Trail Etiquette

The hiking experience includes staying safe and respecting other hikers and the environment.

Stay on Marked Trails: Stay on marked trails to conserve native vegetation and minimize erosion. It also prevents you from getting lost in the outdoors.

Leave No Trace: Remove whatever you brought in, including garbage, leftover food, and other items.

Respect Wildlife: Keep a safe distance from animals, don't feed them, and keep your food secure.

Yield to Others: Be respectful on the trail. Generally, those traveling uphill have the right of way; everyone must yield to horses.

Permit Requirements and Regulations

Most of Sedona's trails are open to the public without requiring a permit, although some locations do, notably for overnight camping or parking at trailheads. Find the most recent information on the Coconino National Forest website or at the Sedona Red Rock Ranger District office. Always follow the posted notice for permits and trail rules.

Furthermore, several culturally sensitive locations surrounding Sedona are protected, and access to them may be limited or need special permission. Respecting these regulations helps to protect Sedona's heritage and natural beauty for future generations.

You can ensure a safe and fun hiking trip in Sedona by planning. Gather the necessary equipment, understand the weather conditions, adhere to safety requirements and trail etiquette, and respect all local restrictions. With these precautions, you're ready to enjoy the stunning landscapes that make Sedona a world-class hiking destination.

Discover Sedona: Easy Trails for Every Beginner

Sedona, located in the heart of Arizona's Red Rock Country, provides a variety of beautiful paths that are both accessible and breathtaking. Sedona, known for its breathtaking vistas, is a haven for hikers of all ability levels, including beginners searching for easy yet rewarding trips. Whether you're looking for a relaxing walk to clear your thoughts or an opportunity to take stunning images, Sedona's novice trails are the ideal introduction to the area's natural splendor. Let's look at some of the top basic trails in Sedona for individuals new to hiking.

Bell Rock Pathway: one of Sedona's most recognizable features, rises boldly with its distinctive bell-shaped form. The Bell Rock Pathway is an easily accessible trail with stunning views and a reasonably flat slope, making it ideal for novices. The walk is approximately 3.6 miles round trip, giving hikers close-up views of Bell Rock and Courthouse Butte without requiring a difficult climb. Interpretive markers along the path provide information on the local vegetation and geology, making this trip both scenic and educational.

Cathedral Rock: While the complete journey up Cathedral Rock is more difficult, the first segment of the Cathedral Rock Trail is a more manageable option that provides breathtaking views. The trail begins at the Cathedral Rock Trailhead and winds through wide views, making it an easy but rewarding climb for beginners. This shorter walk route allows hikers to take in the magnificent scenery of Cathedral Rock and the surrounding terrain without the hard ascent, making it ideal for people with minimal hiking expertise or families with children.

Red Rock Crossing Trail: is a gorgeous and quiet trail that leads to one of Arizona's most photographed views: Cathedral Rock reflected in the waters of Oak Creek. This track is quite flat and provides a pleasant walk through riparian nature, making it ideal for novices and anyone seeking a relaxing hiking experience. The route leads to a gorgeous picnic place by the stream, where the spectacular reflection of Cathedral Rock provides the perfect backdrop for a quiet afternoon.

The West Fork Trail: is one of Sedona's most popular treks, known for its stunning canyon vistas and the shade afforded by dense forest trees. This trail provides a cool break from Sedona's heat, making it excellent for the warmer months. The trip is relatively straightforward, following Oak Creek and crossing it at several points via stepping stones or small footbridges. The track is around 3 miles one way and is well-maintained, allowing beginner hikers to appreciate the beautiful red cliffs and luxuriant flora without any strenuous climbs.

Doe Mountain Trail: For novices seeking a somewhat more difficult trek, Doe Mountain provides a rewarding experience with breathtaking views. The route is a short but steep ascent that ends in a flat mesa with a panoramic view of Sedona's red rock scenery. This climb is around 1.5 miles round trip, and while the ascent may be strenuous, the breathtaking views from the top make it all worthwhile. The walk is well-marked, and the mesa's large, open space at the summit is ideal for meditation, yoga, or simply watching the sunset.

The Jim Thompson Trail: is ideal for people looking for a little bit of everything. It is reasonably flat and provides a variety of views of Sedona's rock formations, including Steamboat Rock and Wilson Mountain. This trail is about 5 miles round trip and winds through manzanita and pinyon pine trees, making it a gorgeous yet not too strenuous hike. It's a fantastic choice for beginners who want to spend more time experiencing Sedona's natural environment without traveling into steep or difficult terrain.

Sedona's basic trails provide an excellent introduction to hiking in one of the most scenic areas in the United States. These paths are intended to accommodate beginners and those seeking a less demanding outdoor experience, ensuring that everyone, regardless of hiking skill, may enjoy the beauty of Sedona. Each route offers unique views of Sedona's red cliffs, rich greenery, and serene water features, making it a special place. So, lace up your hiking boots, bring your water bottle, and prepare to explore Sedona's mild yet breathtaking trails, where each step is an opportunity to find something lovely.

Sedona's Scenic Challenge: Moderate Trails for Experienced Hikers.

Sedona, Arizona, is more than simply a place for spiritual renewal or a stroll among stunning red rock formations; it is also a haven for hikers looking to push themselves on more difficult trails. For every traveler who has gazed at Sedona's natural beauty from the well-trodden trails, a trail awaits to enhance their experience. These moderate trails, ideal for experienced hikers, offer physical challenges, breathtaking views, and a deeper connection to the ecosystem. Consider Sedona's most rewarding moderate routes that appeal to the daring spirit.

Devil's Bridge Trail: is one of Sedona's most photographed natural arches, with a thrilling hike culminating in a spectacular natural sandstone arch that stands out against the Arizona sky. The Devil's Bridge walk is relatively short (4.2 miles round trip) but includes a difficult ascent to the arch itself. This moderate trip is worth the effort because it leads to one of the largest natural arches in the Sedona area, allowing courageous hikers to stroll across the bridge and enjoy the breathtaking views.

Soldier Pass Trail: This 4.5-mile loop is somewhat difficult and rich in natural and historical value. The Soldier Pass Trail leads past the Devil's Kitchen sinkhole and the Seven Sacred Pools, where water pools in a succession of natural rock basins. The trail also includes Soldier Pass Cave, an impressive natural cavern for hikers. This trail combines natural beauty, geological wonders, and some adventure, making it a must-do for those who enjoy hiking with various attractions.

Boynton Canyon Trail: is one of Sedona's most gorgeous places, with towering red rock formations and lush flora. The trail is approximately 6.1 miles roundtrip, providing a moderate hike with some elevation increase. As you progress deeper into the canyon, the road weaves through magnificent wooded landscape and past historic Sinagua cliff homes, considered over 800 years old. The trail's finish provides a breathtaking panoramic view of the canyon, making it a worthwhile climb for anyone who enjoys the natural beauty and historical mystery.

The Airport Mesa Loop: For those wishing to combine a modest climb with some of Sedona's best panoramic views, the Airport Mesa Loop is an excellent option. This 3.5-mile walk encircles the top of Airport Mesa, offering panoramic views of Sedona and its famed red rocks, such as Bell Rock, Cathedral Rock, and Courthouse Butte. The path is well-maintained, although some short, steep parts will test your endurance. Hiking this walk at sunset is particularly lovely, as the departing light produces a warm glow on the red rocks.

Thunder Mountain Trail: Thunder Mountain, Sedona's tallest peak, offers a more remote and hard hike for those wishing to avoid the more popular paths. The trail to the peak is approximately 2.5 kilometers one way and has a major elevation climb. The path is rugged in places, providing a true sense of adventure. Hikers are rewarded with panoramic views of West Sedona and the Verde Valley from the peak, making it an ideal site for quiet isolation or breathtaking photography.

Sedona's moderate trails provide an ideal balance of effort and reward for experienced hikers. Each trail has its distinct mix of natural features and viewpoints, ranging from towering arches and fascinating caves to tranquil canyon depths and exhilarating mountain peaks. These treks test your physical abilities and create a deep connection to the natural environment, representing the daring spirit that pulls many people to Sedona's red rock landscapes. Whether you want privacy, adventure, or just a terrific workout in some of the most magnificent scenery in the Southwest, Sedona's moderate routes will boost your hiking experience.

Sedona's Ultimate Challenge: Trails for Adventure Seekers

Sedona, Arizona, is known not just for its bustling arts scene and spiritual retreats but also for its magnificent red rock landscapes, which provide some of the most strenuous and rewarding hiking trails in the United States. For those who desire adventure and aren't scared of a physical challenge, Sedona's trails provide exhilarating ascents, spectacular views, and the raw beauty of the unspoiled wilderness. These trails are not for the faint of heart but for those who want to push their limitations and experience the roughness of Arizona's environment at its most extreme. Here's a detailed guide to the most strenuous treks in Sedona, where adventurers can challenge their limits.

Bear Mountain Trail: is one of Sedona's most strenuous walks, with minimal shade, steep slopes, and complicated navigation. This climb covers around 5 miles roundway and ascends over 2,000 feet, delivering a rigorous exercise with multiple false summits. The trail is strenuous, but the payoff is unparalleled: panoramic vistas of the Verde Valley, San Francisco Peaks, and Red Rock-Secret Mountain Wilderness. It's a difficult hike, but the sense of accomplishment and breathtaking views at the top are well worth the effort.

The Hangover Trail: is well-known for its distinctive path that follows the side of a cliff, providing thrilling panoramas and heart-pounding stretches through Sedona's famed red rocks. This 8.2-mile loop is physically and technically difficult, necessitating good route-finding abilities and a head for heights. The hike offers beautiful views of Munds Wagon, Cow Pies, and Merry-Go-Round Rock. Experienced hikers seeking an adrenaline rush and superb photo opportunities will find this trek unforgettable.

Wilson Mountain Trail: As Sedona's highest peak, Wilson Mountain provides one of the more difficult walks in the area. The trail is about 10 miles round trip and climbs around 2,500 feet. Hikers can choose between the north and south trailheads, which provide diverse views and terrains. The summit of Wilson Mountain offers panoramic views of the whole Sedona Valley, including Oak Creek Canyon and the red rock buttes below. This climb requires a full day and rewards hikers with some of northern Arizona's most stunning views.

The Aerie to Cockscomb Loop: is approximately 10 miles long and offers a variety of sceneries ranging from deep woodlands to wide desert terrains. This trail loop is recognized for its elevation fluctuations and difficult terrain, making it ideal for those seeking diversity and challenge. The path passes Doe Mountain and Bear Mountain, giving you plenty of opportunities to experience Sedona's geological diversity and sweeping vistas.

The journey to Cathedral Rock via the Templeton Trail and Baldwin Loop is a strenuous climb with some rough parts requiring scrambling. While not as long as other treks, the steep rise and descent are an excellent workout, and the trail offers beautiful views of Cathedral Rock from various angles. The track is approximately 7 miles long when paired with the Baldwin Loop, which skirts around Oak Creek and provides a nice change of scenery and an opportunity to cool off.

The Secret Canyon Trail: located in the heart of the Red Rock-Secret Mountain Wilderness, is a tough 10-mile hike that takes you deep into a lonely canyon. This trail is less frequented, providing a sense of remoteness and raw wildness. It is ideal for adventurers who love the tranquility of nature while embarking on a physically difficult walk. The trail is relatively undeveloped and requires navigation skills, especially since it can get overgrown or obstructed by fallen trees and other natural obstructions.

Sedona's tough routes provide serious hikers with the ultimate outdoor encounter. These hikes are far from easy—they need physical stamina, skillful footwork, and an adventurous spirit. Each trail has its mix of challenges and rewards, offering even the most experienced hikers with unforgettable experiences in Arizona's red rock area. Whether you're climbing Bear Mountain or walking the cliffside trails of Hangover Trail, Sedona's difficult treks provide both the excitement of the climb and the ultimate in natural beauty.

Cathedral Rock: A Spiritual Journey Through Sedona's Red Rocks.

Cathedral Rock, nestled amid Arizona's spectacular Red Rock Country, is more than simply a stunning geological structure; it's a beacon for people seeking spiritual rejuvenation and a symbol of Sedona's natural beauty, which draws many pilgrims. Cathedral Rock, which rises dramatically from the ground to form a massive red sandstone edifice, is more than just a beautiful marvel; it is also a spiritual touchstone that attracts travelers worldwide. This tour explores the trek to and around Cathedral Rock, providing insights into its remarkable impact on all who visit.

Geology of Cathedral Rock.

Cathedral Rock is primarily made of Permian Schnebly Hill sandstone, notable for its vivid red hues that shine brightly at sunrise and sunset. Erosion has molded this formation over millions of years, resulting in the remarkable vertical fissures and buttresses that give the rock its cathedral aspect. The rock is not only a geological wonder but also serves as the focal point of Sedona's panoramic view, dominating the area with its powerful presence.

Hike to Cathedral Rock

Reaching the summit of Cathedral Rock is a route that appeals to people who are physically fit and prepared for a moderate to difficult hike. The trail to the top is roughly 1.2 miles roundway, but it includes a hard rise over granite that necessitates scrambling and cautious navigation. Despite the physical strain, hikers are rewarded with one of Sedona's most breathtaking views—the panoramic vistas from the saddle of Cathedral Rock.

The hike begins at the Cathedral Rock Trailhead off Back O'Beyond Road. The route gradually steepens as you ascend, providing early glimpses of the magnificence that awaits. The last ascent is climbing up rock faces utilizing natural footholds and crevices—a thrilling challenge that adds to the sensation of accomplishment once at the peak.

Spiritual Significance

Cathedral Rock is said to be the site of a powerful energy vortex—a location where the earth's energy is concentrated and felt more strongly. Many people feel that vortexes encourage healing, meditation, and self-discovery. Visitors frequently come to Cathedral Rock to meditate, do yoga, or simply sit and soak up the peaceful vibe of the surroundings.

Cathedral Rock is reported to have feminine energy, which promotes virtues such as compassion, gentleness, and patience. It's a place where many people sense a stronger connection to the land and a better balance with the universe. Whether one believes in vortexes, Cathedral Rock's tranquility and breathtaking beauty provide an ideal backdrop for introspection and renewal.

Photography & Art

Cathedral Rock is one of Sedona's most photographed attractions. Its unmistakable silhouette against the sky makes it a popular subject for photographers and artists, who capture its varied moods in various lighting circumstances. Sunset is especially stunning as the rocks change from blazing red to muted tones of purple, producing a dreamlike sight that appears almost extraterrestrial.

Conservation efforts

Preserving Cathedral Rock and its surroundings is a priority for the Sedona community and visitors. Maintaining the route and adjacent surroundings helps to ensure that this natural treasure continues to inspire future generations. Hikers are expected to follow Leave No Trace principles, packing out everything they bring in and staying on authorized trails to reduce their influence on the delicate desert ecology.

A visit to Cathedral Rock is more than just a hike; it's a pilgrimage to one of the world's most magnificent natural cathedrals. Whether the climb's difficulty lures you, the promise of spiritual enlightenment, or simply the opportunity to observe stunning natural beauty, Cathedral Rock provides a deep experience that will last long after the physical trek is completed. It serves as a memorial not just to the geological forces that molded it but also to the eternal human spirit that seeks connection with something larger amidst our world's natural beauty.

Bell Rock Pathway: Exploring Iconic Views in Sedona's Red Rock Wonderland

Bell Rock is a colossal beacon in Sedona, Arizona's breathtaking landscape, attracting visitors with its distinctive, bell-shaped form. The Bell Rock Pathway is more than a hike; it's an experience through some of Sedona's most renowned landscapes, combining physical exertion, stunning scenery, and an undeniable sense of tranquility. This guide explores the Bell Rock Pathway, showing why it's a must-see for anybody visiting Sedona, whether for hiking, photography, or spiritual renewal.

A Geological Marvel

Like much of Sedona, Bell Rock is primarily made up of red sandstone formations that date back millions of years. These formations were formed by layers of sandstone and limestone worn by the environment, resulting in the distinctive landscapes that make Sedona a geological wonderland. The rock is named for its unusual bell shape and is one of the most clearly identifiable features in the area.

Hike the Bell Rock Pathway.

The Bell Rock Pathway is an easily accessible trail that welcomes hikers of all ability levels to explore the great outdoors. The walk, around 3.6 miles round trip, is reasonably flat, making it suited for beginners while rewarding more experienced hikers due to the beautiful views it provides.

Beginning in the north at the Bell Rock Vista and Pathway parking area, the walk meanders towards Bell Rock and Courthouse Butte, another remarkable rock structure nearby. The trail is well-maintained and easy to navigate, providing up-close views of Sedona's red rock backdrop.

As hikers travel down the trail, they come across various spurs that lead closer to Bell Rock. Those feeling daring can scramble up Bell Rock's lower slopes. These routes are more difficult and require some climbing, but they provide an exciting experience and even better views of the surrounding area.

Photographic Opportunities

The Bell Rock Pathway is a photographers' paradise. The trail offers various opportunities to capture the breathtaking scenery of Sedona. Morning and late afternoon are especially magical times to photograph Bell Rock because the changing light bathes it in rich, golden hues or casts dramatic shadows, highlighting its distinct shapes. Seasonal changes also bring a variety of hues, such as spring wildflowers or summer vegetation, which lend depth and contrast to the red rocks.

Spiritual and Recreational Appeal

Many travelers come to Bell Rock for its physical beauty and spiritual allure. The region surrounding Bell Rock is said to be an energy vortex, making it a popular spot for individuals seeking meditation, spiritual reflection, or simply a profound sense of tranquility in nature. The energy here is claimed to be conducive to healing and transformation, which draws visitors worldwide.

Aside from its spiritual appeal, the Bell Rock Pathway is popular with cyclists and runners due to its wide, smooth routes. The pathway connects to other trails in the Sedona area, providing longer paths for those who want to explore further.

Conservation and Respect for Nature

Like all of Sedona's natural landmarks, Bell Rock encourages visitors to practice responsible tourism. This involves following the Leave No Trace principles, such as staying on authorized trails, removing all waste, and not disrupting the natural flora and fauna. These approaches ensure that this great natural treasure is preserved for future generations.

The Bell Rock Pathway captures the heart of Sedona: its natural beauty, spiritual significance, and outdoor recreation choices. Hiking this trail allows you to connect with nature, challenge yourself physically, and perhaps find calm in the breathtaking red rock environment. For many, a visit to Bell Rock is more than just a walk; it is a voyage into the heart of one of the most breathtakingly spectacular sites on the planet. Whether seen via a camera lens, exploring on foot, or soaked in its spiritual essence, Bell Rock is a monument to Sedona's ageless beauty.

Soldier Pass Trail: Caves, Arches, and Pools in Sedona's Red Rocks

The Soldier Pass Trail, located in the heart of Arizona's Red Rock Country, offers a one-of-a-kind combination of natural beauty and historical significance, making it one of Sedona's most exciting treks. This trail is more than just a route through the woods; it's a trip through time, revealing geological wonders and remnants of old human history. Soldier Pass has fascinating tunnels, natural arches, and sacred waters. This comprehensive guide goes into the climb, highlighting each key feature and explaining why Soldier Pass is a must-see for any adventurer in Sedona.

The Trail Begins

Soldier Pass Trail is relatively mild, covering around 4.5 miles round trip. It begins at the Soldier Pass Trailhead, located in a quiet residential section of Sedona, limiting parking access and forcing hikers to start early in the day. The walk rapidly immerses you in Sedona's breathtaking surroundings, which include towering red rock formations that change color with the sun.

Remarkable Features of the Soldier Pass

The Devil's Kitchen Sinkhole is the trail's first major feature, a vast natural depression that has grown due to natural erosion. The collapse of subsurface limestone caverns causes Sedona's largest sinkhole. Observing the sinkhole provides a striking visual representation of the geological processes at work under Sedona's surface.

Hikers continue down the trail until they reach the Seven Sacred Pools, a series of natural pools carved into the rock that collect rainwater and runoff. Many consider these pools sacred, highlighting the spiritual value of natural water sources in parched regions. The pools are especially beautiful after a rainstorm, reflecting the sky and neighboring cliffs in their calm waters.

The most exciting aspect of Soldier Pass is the cave, which is located off the main trail and requires some scrambling to reach. Soldier Pass Cave is a large cave carved into the soft sandstone, providing shade and a moment of rest for hikers.

Inside, the cave gives a cool, peaceful spot to think on the journey while enjoying the natural acoustics of this secret chamber.

Another amazing natural creation is the Soldier Pass Arch near the cave. This arch is a stunning example of wind and water erosion, with a perfect framing that reveals views of the sky and mountains beyond. It's a popular destination for photographers looking to capture the essence of Sedona's geological artistry.

Flora & Fauna Along the Way

The region's unique plants and fauna are on full display as you walk the trail. Juniper trees and prickly pear cacti grow in the area, and fauna such as mule deer, coyotes, and various birds can occasionally be spotted. Spring delivers a burst of color as wildflowers bloom over the countryside, adding to the trail's visual appeal.

Historical context and Spiritual significance

The Soldier Pass area has a rich history, having been used by Native American tribes and later by settlers and the military, hence its name. The trail and landmarks are rich in tales and spiritual mythology; many consider them centers of power and energy. This spiritual aspect attracts many tourists looking to connect with the land on a deeper level.

Hiking Tips and Conservation

To appreciate the Soldier Pass Trail, you must be well-equipped. Here are some suggestions for potential hikers:

- Start early to ensure parking and avoid the midday heat.
- Carry plenty of water, as the terrain has limited shade.
- Wear hiking footwear suitable for the rugged and often slippery terrain.
- Respect the trail and its natural and cultural aspects by adhering to established trails and following Leave No Trace principles.

Soldier Pass Trail is more than just a hike; it takes you into Sedona's natural and spiritual heart. Hikers are greeted with incredible scenery with each step, from gigantic sinkholes and tranquil lakes to secret caves and framing arches. It's a location where the past and present collide, and the soul of the land communicates with people who tread its paths.

Soldier Pass promises a journey of discovery and awe, whether you're an avid hiker searching for a challenge, a nature lover looking for beauty, or a seeker of serenity.

Devil's Bridge: A Magnificent Journey Through Sedona's Iconic Landscape.

Devil's Bridge is one of Sedona's most impressive natural sights. This beautiful sandstone arch, etched by erosion, is a remarkable example of natural architecture that draws hikers worldwide. The journey to Devil's Bridge is a physical challenge and a visual spectacle, with panoramic views and a sense of accomplishment that appeals to all visitors. This thorough examination delves into the hiking experience, geological significance, and magnificent beauty of Devil's Bridge.

Introduction to Devil's Bridge.

Devil's Bridge is Arizona's most significant natural sandstone arch in the Red Rock Secret Mountain Wilderness near Sedona. It rises majestically, framing the azure sky and creating an almost dreamlike setting. The Bridge resulted from millions of years of wind and water erosion, which worked together to build this natural beauty. The moniker

'Devil's Bridge' evokes curiosity and a sense of mystery, adding to the appeal that lures eager explorers to this location.

Hike to Devil's Bridge

The walk to Devil's Bridge is one of Sedona's most popular climbs, recognized for its breathtaking splendor and the satisfying experience of stepping on the Bridge. The trailhead is accessible from Dry Creek Road, and the hike is relatively modest, making it appropriate for most fitness levels.

Trail Details: The total round trip distance is roughly 4.2 miles, with the final half of the journey featuring a hard elevation to the arch. The path is well-kept, with good markings and explanatory signs directing walkers across the various terrain.

Scenic Route: As you go along the path, the terrain changes from high desert plants, such as juniper and cactus, to breathtaking rock formations that capture the essence of the American Southwest. The trail's colors change with the light, with shades of red, orange, and gold that are especially spectacular at sunrise and dusk.

Climbing to the Arch: The last trek to Devil's Bridge involves some cautious stepping and light climbing, but it is doable for people with a modest fitness level. This hike section is thrilling, as each step brings you closer to the breathtaking stone edifice.

Standing on the Devil's Bridge

The experience of standing on Devil's Bridge is one of thrill and amazement. The arch is wide enough to feel secure, yet the open sides provide an exhilarating sensation of exposure. The views from atop the Bridge are panoramic, highlighting Sedona's vast wilderness, with layers of mountains and valleys stretching into the distance. It's an ideal location for photography, meditation, or simply taking in the grand splendor of the countryside.

Geological Significance.

Devil's Bridge is a tribute to the lasting power of natural erosion. The arch is made chiefly of Permian Age sandstone, known as the Schnebly Hill Formation. This type of rock is common throughout Sedona and is recognized for its toughness and vivid red hue, enhanced at sunrise and sunset.

The development of Devil's Bridge is a superb example of how even the most potent rock can be shaped by nature's persistent forces, resulting in forms that inspire and amaze.

Conservation efforts

The popularity of Devil's Bridge entails a responsibility to maintain its beauty and purity. Local conservation groups and the US Forest Service work together to keep the route and neighboring regions in good condition, safeguarding the natural ecology and ensuring that future generations enjoy this spectacular place. Hikers are asked to follow Leave No Trace principles, which include packing out all litter, staying on designated routes, and respecting wildlife.

A visit to Devil's Bridge is more than simply a stroll; it's an immersion into Sedona's red rock area. The trek to the Bridge is brimming with natural beauty, from the rich vegetation and spectacular rock formations to the majestic finale of standing atop one of nature's most magnificent arches. Devil's Bridge is more than a location; it's an experience that captures Sedona's adventurous attitude, geological history, and panoramic beauty. Whether you're a seasoned hiker or a casual adventurer, the route to Devil's Bridge promises to be one of the most unforgettable experiences in this renowned terrain.

Boynton Canyon: Exploring Energy Vortexes and Ancient Echoes

Boynton Canyon, located in the heart of Sedona's spectacular red rock region, is a location that is more than simply visually stunning; it is also rich in history, mysticism, and mystery. This breathtaking canyon, known for its energy vortexes and relics of ancient houses, provides tourists with a one-of-a-kind opportunity to connect with both the past and themselves. Boynton Canyon is a tapestry of nature and human history waiting to be discovered, from mystical energy centers thought to aid in healing and meditation to silent stone structures left by previous civilizations.

The Spiritual and Natural Beauty of Boynton Canyon

The Boynton Canyon hike is one of Sedona's most beautiful and spiritually enlightening experiences. The walk, around 6.1 miles round-trip, leads deep into the canyon, past towering cliffs and lush vegetation that changes with the seasons. The trek is relatively difficult, delivering a rewarding physical adventure that parallels the metaphysical discovery many seek in this venerated location.

Energy vortexes: Gateways to Enlightenment.

Boynton Canyon is known for its energy vortexes, which are swirling centers of energy that promote healing, meditation, and self-discovery. These vortexes are thought to be the consequence of natural electromagnetic ground energies that occur at specific spots around Sedona, with Boynton Canyon housing one of the most powerful. Visitors frequently describe experiencing increased spiritual and emotional clarity when near these vortexes, making Boynton Canyon a favorite location for individuals seeking personal enlightenment and a greater connection with nature.

Ancient Dwellings and Echoes from the Past

As you progress deeper into the canyon, the trail leads to historic cliff houses that date back over a thousand years. The Sinagua, an indigenous people who lived in the region between 500 and 1425 AD, erected these constructions. The residences are made of stone and lie precariously under overhangs in the canyon walls, shielded from the weather but wholly incorporated into the scenery. Exploring these ancient ruins provides visitors with a unique view into the daily life of Sinagua, whose legacy in the red rocks of Sedona is both humbling and uplifting.

Plants and wildlife: Life among the rocks.

Boynton Canyon's biological diversity adds to its attraction. The walk begins in a sparse high desert scrub area, but as you climb the canyon, the scenery changes to a lush riparian zone. This area is home to tall hardwoods, evergreen bushes, and a diverse range of species, including deer, coyotes, and birds. Spring delivers brilliant wildflowers, while fall cloaks the canyon in fiery hues, adding to the mysterious mood of the journey.

Hiking and Preservation Tips

To fully appreciate and respect the beauty of Boynton Canyon, hikers are asked to observe these guidelines:

Prepare for the Trail: Bring enough water, wear appropriate footwear, and sun protection, as the Arizona heat can be fierce even in the cooler months.

Respect the Land: Stick to approved routes to help protect the fragile desert habitat and the integrity of the ancient structures.

Embrace Silence: Boynton Canyon is a site of natural beauty and historic significance. Visitors are encouraged to keep noise and technology distractions to a minimum to enhance their and others' experiences.

Leave No Trace: Remove any rubbish and leave anything you find, including rocks, plants, and artifacts. The homes and artifacts are protected by federal law and cannot be damaged.

Boynton Canyon is more than just a beautiful hike; it's an adventure through time, energy, and spirituality. Whether pulled by the call of its ancient houses, the magnetism of its energy vortexes, or simply the breathtaking natural beauty, travelers find Boynton Canyon a meaningful connection to the past and a calm haven for personal meditation. The gentle murmurs of the wind in the canyon, as well as the breathtaking panoramas that reveal along the walk, serve as a timeless reminder to explore, preserve, and protect this magnificent corner of the globe.

Explore Sedona: Special Interest Hiking Adventures

Sedona, Arizona, a treasure trove of picturesque trails and natural wonders, is a paradise for passionate hikers and an ideal location for special interest excursions. Sedona has a trail for everyone, whether you're a family looking for an accessible outdoor adventure, a pet owner looking to share the experience with your furry friend, a nature lover looking to witness breathtaking sunrises and sunsets, or a geology enthusiast eager to learn about the earth'sEarth's ancient stories. This book delves deeply into the family-friendly hikes, pet-friendly paths, greatest sites for celestial observations, and geological wonders that make hiking in Sedona an unforgettable experience.

Family-Friendly Hikes

Fay Canyon Trail: is a good trek for families because it is generally flat and just over a mile long, making it accessible to hikers of all ages. The trail is shaded by towering cliffs and rich flora, offering a refreshing reprieve even in hot weather.

Along the journey, there are fantastic rock formations and an optional rock scramble to a natural arch, which provides a fun challenge for children and an excellent photo opportunity for parents.

Bell Rock Pathway: This trail provides an easy hike with the option of going further and higher depending on the family's hiking ability. The trail offers beautiful views of Bell Rock and Courthouse Butte. Its wide and well-maintained track is excellent for strollers, provided you stick to the lower sections and many places to stop and take in the landscape.

Red Rock State Park: is family-friendly, with various accessible trails, educational events, and guided nature hikes. The park's visitor center contains a wealth of information on the surrounding flora and wildlife, and park rangers provide regular enjoyable and educational activities, making it an educational visit for youngsters.

Pet-friendly trails

West Fork Trail: one of Sedona's most popular treks, is also pet-friendly, with leashed dogs allowed to splash in Oak Creek and explore the beautiful, tree-lined road alongside their owners. This trail provides shade and water—a welcome reprieve for pets on hot days—and breathtaking canyon vistas that change with the seasons.

Baldwin Trail: begins at Cathedral Rock and is a relatively easy loop that enables leashed pets. The trail has river access points so pets can cool down, and the open vistas provide several photo opportunities for pet owners. The varied landscape makes the trek enjoyable for both humans and animals.

Mescal Mountain Loop: For more adventurous pets and their humans, Mescal Mountain provides a moderate track with wide trails and slight elevation rise. The trail is recognized for its breathtaking views of the surrounding desert and rock formations, making it an enjoyable experience for pet-friendly hikers.

Best Sunrise and Sunset Spots

Airport Mesa: is a fantastic location for dawn or sunset, as it is easily accessible and has one of the best panoramic views of Sedona. The view spans much of the city and the surrounding red cliffs, with changing light dramatically affecting the environment.

Cathedral Rock: The sunset views from Cathedral Rock are unrivaled for those prepared to take a moderate hike. The approach can be complex, but the location offers one of Sedona's most iconic sunset views, with the rock formations blazing spectacularly in the setting sun.

Doe Mountain Trail: is a short but steep trek to Doe Mountain's flat mesa top, offering 360-degree vistas ideal for sunrise and sunset watchers. The panoramic vista includes views of Bear Mountain, Boynton Canyon, and the distant peaks surrounding Sedona.

The Geological Wonders of Sedona

Devil's Bridge: is Sedona's most incredible natural sandstone arch and provides insight into the geological forces shaping the area. The climb to the Bridge is widespread, and the final vista of the arch is a breathtaking example of natural building.

Amitabha Stupa and Peace Park: While not a trek Amitabha Stupa and Peace Park provide a geological and spiritual experience where tourists can view the red rock formations while meditating and feeling at peace. The region is surrounded by magnificent red rocks that create a peaceful setting for reflection.

Palatki Heritage Site: is home to ancient Sinagua cliff dwellings and rock art, making for a historical and geological trip. The red rock cliffs at the site have a variety of geological layers and shapes, which provide information on the area's natural history and human occupancy.

More than merely a nature walk, Sedona's trails serve as a portal to excursions tailored to specific interests. Whether your priority is family-friendly accessibility, pet accommodation, capturing the ideal sunrise or sunset, or exploring ancient geological formations, Sedona's diverse landscape offers an unforgettable outdoor experience tailored to your preferences. Each trail tests the body and stimulates the mind and spirit, making every hike in Sedona a memorable experience.

Sedona's Seasonal Hiking Guide: Accepting Nature's Rhythms

Sedona, Arizona, is known not just for its distinctive red rocks and spiritual vortexes but also for the unique experiences it provides with each season. The terrain evolves each season, bringing fresh hues, temperatures, and obstacles, making Sedona a year-round hiking destination. From the brilliant blossoms of spring to the tranquil snowscapes of winter, hiking in Sedona is a never-ending adventure. This detailed book delves into what each season brings to the trails, ensuring your hiking experience is safe and memorable.

Spring: Wildflowers and Cacti Bloom

Springtime in Sedona is a festival of life and color. As the temperatures rise in late February and March, the environment comes alive with the brilliant colors of wildflowers and cacti blossoms. This is ideal for photographers and wildlife enthusiasts to hit the trails.

Best trails for spring blooms

Cathedral Rock Trail: This intermediate climb not only provides breathtaking views of one of Sedona's most iconic rock formations but also includes an abundance of wildflowers along the creek in early spring.

Brins Mesa Trail: Brins Mesa bursts with color following a wet winter. The walk is perfect for observing high desert wildflowers and the spectacular spread of cactus blooms that dot the landscape.

What to Look For

Timing is everything in spring. Blooms can change from year to year based on rainfall and temperature. Late March to early May is usually the optimum time to see this desert transition.

Rattlesnakes and other creatures become more active as temperatures rise. Be cautious on the trails, particularly in natural regions with dense undergrowth or near water sources.

Summer: Monsoons and Night Hikes

Sedona's summer heat is broken up by the dramatic monsoon season, which usually begins in July and lasts until early September. These storms bring pleasant rains and lower temperatures, making late afternoons and evenings perfect for hiking.

The best trails for summer evenings

Airport Loop Trail: Known for its breathtaking sunset views, this trail is a reasonably moderate hike that is ideal for enjoying the spectacular skies and lower temps of a rainy evening.

Doe Mountain Trail: With a vast mesa top, Doe Mountain is ideal for a night trek. The top offers 360-degree vistas that are incredibly stunning when illuminated by a full moon.

What to Look For

Monsoon safety is crucial. Keep a close eye on the weather, as flash floods and lightning are potential threats. Plan to begin hikes early in the day and leave the trails by the afternoon, when storms generally sweep in.

Night hiking necessitates adequate preparedness. Bring headlamps and additional clothing, and make sure you know the terrain or hike with a guide.

Autumn: Colors and Cooler Trails

As the heat of summer fades, autumn brings a cooler, quieter time to explore Sedona. The changing foliage and pleasant temps make October the finest time for trekking.

Best Trails for Fall Colors

West Fork Trail: This is Sedona's signature autumn hike. The trail leads you through a canopy of trees along a stream bed, with golden yellow and flaming red foliage contrasting nicely with the red rock walls.

Boynton Canyon Trail: In the fall, this trail is an excellent area to witness the changing colors of the leaves blended with the evergreen junipers and pines and the fantastic red rock views.

What to Look For

Weather can be unpredictable, with warm days and cool nights. Layering your clothing allows you to adjust comfortably while hiking.

Wildlife is particularly active as it prepares for winter, so stay alert and respectful, especially at dawn and dusk.

Winter: Snow-capped Red Rocks

Winter transforms Sedona's landscape into a peaceful, mystical world of snow-capped rocks and clear skies. While snowfall is typically tiny and sporadic, it lends a wonderful touch to the red rocks, providing a fresh perspective on the pathways.

Best Trails for Winter Hiking

Bell Rock Pathway: This trail is open most of the winter and provides beautiful Bell Rock and Courthouse Butte vistas, especially with a sprinkling of snow.

Bear Mountain Trail: For the most daring, Bear Mountain offers a strenuous hike with breathtaking views of the snow-dusted red cliffs. Prepare for freezing conditions and strenuous hiking.

What to Look For

Trails can be slick, and snow can hide trail markings. It is critical to wear adequate footwear, utilize trekking poles for support, and hike in groups.

Winter storms can swiftly affect trail conditions, so check weather forecasts on a frequent basis.

Sedona is a year-round destination for hikers exploring the natural world, with each season bringing its unique beauty and challenges. Whether you're watching the colorful blooms of spring, the spectacular summer monsoons, the quiet beauty of fall, or the serene landscapes of winter, Sedona provides a profound connection to nature that rejuvenates the spirit while challenging the body.

Sedona: An Exploration of History, Culture, and Nature

Sedona, Arizona, is well-known for its breathtaking red rock formations, outdoor adventure activities, and rich cultural and historical legacy. This high-desert terrain has been altered by ancient civilizations, settlers, and, most recently, tourists seeking to experience its distinctive beauty. From its beginnings as a gathering spot for indigenous tribes to its current status as a top destination for outdoor enthusiasts, Sedona's history is as deep and complicated as the rock formations that characterize it. This essay dives into the history of hiking in Sedona, the importance of Native American historical sites, and modern tourism's impact on this beautiful area.

History of Hiking in Sedona

While Sedona's image as a hiking destination is relatively new, exploring the region's trails is much older. Sedona was a sacred site for Native American tribes who lived in and around the area long before it became famed for its outdoor recreation.

Early Indigenous Footprints

Native American groups like the Sinagua, Yavapai, and Apache were the first humans to settle in Sedona. These groups survived in the Sedona area for millennia, relying on the region's natural resources to sustain their societies. Archaeological evidence suggests that the Sinagua people, particularly, built cliff homes and petroglyphs along the canyon walls, many of which are still visible today. These ancient people were deeply connected to the land, constructing trails across the harsh terrain for everyday use, trade, and spiritual purposes.

While the exact purpose of these early routes is unknown, it is evident that they were vital to their way of life, connecting key spots such as water supplies, hunting grounds, and ritual sites. Many of these old roads intersect with modern hiking trails in the region, connecting modern hikers to the same landscapes that indigenous people initially explored.

The Evolution of Hiking Trails in the Modern Period

The first documented usage of hiking as a recreational activity in Sedona occurred in the late nineteenth and early twentieth century. In 1902, the area had its first significant settlement, led by a pioneer named T.C. O'Leary, who noticed its beauty and believed it might be a source of income and tourism. Visitors began to flock to Sedona as the town flourished, drawn by its breathtaking scenery and warm climate.

Outdoor activities like hiking, horseback riding, and camping gained popularity in the early 1900s among people who had come to the area to escape the heat of the lower desert regions. These early pioneers and adventurers created many of Sedona's earliest hiking paths. These folks, including artists and photographers, mapped paths through the vast canyons, rock formations, and riverbeds, many of which are still used as the foundation for modern trails in the area.

As the town became an outdoor adventure destination, hiking was formally added to the area's tourism offerings. By the mid-twentieth century, well-established paths such as the

Cathedral Rock Trail, the West Fork Trail, and the Bell Rock Pathway had been thoroughly surveyed, cementing Sedona's reputation as a premier hiking destination. Hiking's incorporation into the tourism environment has developed dramatically, with hundreds of miles of trails now available to visitors, offering a distinct viewpoint on Sedona's spectacular geological characteristics.

Native American Heritage Sites.

Sedona's link to Native American history is reflected in the numerous heritage sites dispersed throughout the area. These sacred sites are more than just a part of Sedona's history; they are still cultural and spiritual centers for many Native American groups.

The Sinagua people

The Sinagua people, who lived in the Sedona area from roughly 500 AD until 1425 AD, are among the most well-known groups. The Sinagua built their homes into the canyon walls, utilizing the natural rock formations for shelter. The remnants of their cliff homes can still be seen today, particularly at Palatki Heritage Site and V Bar V Heritage Site.

These ancient remains provide insight into the Sinagua's daily existence and connection to the Earth.

Visitors to Palatki may tour cliff homes and view some of the region's best-preserved petroglyphs, which are said to depict the Sinagua people's spiritual beliefs, trade routes, and daily activities. Similarly, the V Bar V Heritage Site contains some of Arizona's most notable petroglyphs, with markings believed to symbolize ancient legends and spiritual rituals.

Ceremonial Sites and Energy Vortexes

In addition to archaeological monuments, Sedona is famous for its energy vortexes, which are considered spiritual power centers where Earth's energy is focused. Many Native American tribes, notably the Hopi and Zuni, revere these vortexes, which may be seen in locations such as Boynton Canyon and Airport Mesa. While the specific purpose of these sites is still debated, they remain a focal point for spiritual practices such as meditation and prayer.

These spiritual spots allow modern hikers to connect with something larger than themselves, in addition to physical discovery. The mix of natural beauty, ancient history, and spiritual significance makes these pathways and sites deeply touching for visitors.

Tribal Perspectives on Cultural Preservation

Modern Native American populations in the Southwest, such as the Hopi, Navajo, and Zuni tribes, maintain strong ties to the Sedona area, regarding it as sacred and significant to their cultural legacy. Many tribal communities prioritize the preservation of these artistic and spiritual locations, and they continue to collaborate with local governments and environmental organizations to conserve their ancestral territories.

Many Sedona excursions, hikes, and cultural activities are aimed to emphasize and respect the ancient practices and beliefs that molded the area's past.

The Effect of Tourism on Sedona

Sedona's emergence as a popular tourist destination has resulted in economic prosperity and problems. Over the last few decades, the town has grown from a small, rural community to a thriving destination for visitors worldwide. While tourism has created jobs and boosted the local economy, it has also prompted worries about protecting Sedona's natural and cultural assets.

Sedona's tourism industry has grown significantly, particularly over the previous 20 years. People from many walks of life have been drawn to the region because of its easy access to outdoor adventures and its mystical reputation as a spiritual hub. Visitors visit for several reasons, including hiking, meditation, photography, and simply experiencing the area's distinct atmosphere.

However, the increase in tourism has not been without its drawbacks. The trails, once infrequently traveled, have become busier, particularly during peak seasons such as spring and fall. Popular tourist destinations such as Cathedral Rock, Devil's Bridge, and Boynton Canyon can become overcrowded, prompting worries about the environmental impact of increased foot traffic. Overusing the area has resulted in trail erosion, plant degradation, and wildlife habitat disruption.

Environmental preservation efforts

Recognizing these problems, local governments, environmental organizations, and Sedona citizens have made initiatives to protect the town's natural beauty for future generations. One notable project has been the formation of the Sedona Red Rock Trail Fund, which strives to preserve and improve hiking trails, limit the impact of human activities, and restore damaged ecosystems. In addition, several of Sedona's popular trails now demand permits or have limited access during busy seasons to help control the amount of visitors.

To address the misuse of some regions, efforts have been made to diversify the routes available to tourists. New routes that take hikers off the beaten path are being constructed to help ease crowding at significant destinations and encourage people to explore less heavily visited terrain areas.

Cultural sensitivity and preservation

The tourism boom has also inspired an emphasis on cultural sensitivity. As more people visit Sedona's historical and spiritual sites, there is a rising understanding of respecting the traditions and heritage of the Native American populations that live here. Many local tour guides emphasize the need to respect sacred sites, and some routes even include information on the area's cultural heritage, ensuring that tourists understand the value of the ground they are walking on.

Balancing Economic Growth and Preservation.

Sedona's predicament is not unique; many other popular natural sites worldwide struggle to balance the economic benefits of tourism with the necessity for environmental and cultural preservation. However, Sedona is in a unique position to set an example. Through ethical tourism practices, community involvement, and strong environmental policies, the town can keep its allure while maintaining its unique features.

Sedona's rich history and culture, paired with its breathtaking natural beauty, provide tourists with a multifaceted experience that is both informative and transforming. From the ancient cliff homes of Sinagua to the vibrant spiritual traditions linked to the area's energy vortexes, Sedona has much to offer anyone who can explore its landscapes and hear its stories. The expansion of tourism in Sedona has undoubtedly presented new issues. Still, with careful planning, respect for cultural heritage, and a focus on conservation, Sedona may continue to thrive as a destination that celebrates its history while looking forward.

Historic Sites Along the Trails of Sedona

Sedona, Arizona, a landscape molded by wind and water over millions of years, is more than simply a picturesque beauty; it is also a historically significant place, with history engraved into each route and rock formation. Sedona's trails are more than just pathways through red rock country; they are time capsules that glimpse the lives of Native American tribes, pioneers, and settlers who once roamed this magnificent area.

Ancient Dwellers: Native American History

Before becoming a popular destination for spiritual seekers and outdoor enthusiasts, Sedona was home to several Native American tribes, including the Sinagua, Anasazi, and later the Apache and Yavapai. The trails around Sedona lead to several notable sites that reveal how these cultures lived and interacted with the land.

The Palatki Heritage Site: located in the Coconino National Forest, has cliff dwellings and rock art thought to date back to the Sinagua culture. The site's red rock alcoves include ancient houses that are impressively preserved, directly linking to the region's first occupants. Hiking to this site gives both a physical challenge and an educational excursion through the indigenous Puebloan lifestyle.

Honanki Ruins: like Palatki, are examples of the Sinagua culture's innovative cliff homes. The site features several rooms cut into the cliffs and enormous pictographs on the rock walls, some of which are thought to be over a thousand years old. These photographs depict stories of survival, spiritual beliefs, and daily life, presenting visitors with engaging stories.

The V-Bar-V Heritage Site: is the most known petroglyph site in the Verde Valley, surrounded by the grandeur of red rock country. The Sinagua created this rock art, which portrays animals, human figures, and abstract symbols, providing a glimpse into their society's spiritual and temporal components.

Pioneers and Settlers: The Euro-American Influence.

In the mid to late nineteenth century, Euro-American explorers and settlers arrived in Sedona, each putting their stamp on the landscape. The Munds Wagon Trail and the Jim Thompson Trail are historical routes these early settlers used for logging, grazing, and transportation between Sedona and the surrounding areas.

Pioneers initially used the Munds Wagon Trail to transport cattle between summer pastures on the Mogollon Rim and winter range in the Verde Valley. It was eventually adapted for wagon traffic. Today, it is a picturesque climb that provides breathtaking vistas and teaches visitors about the area's ranching history. Interpretive plaques along the trail explain the early settlers' trials and innovations.

The Jim Thompson Trail, named after Jim Thompson, Sedona's first permanent European-American inhabitant, was part of the initial wagon route into the area. Hiking this trail is like going through a chapter of Sedona's pioneer history, with paths that meander through locations rich in stories from the early twentieth century.

Military Outposts and Historical Structures

Fort Apache, however, a little further from Sedona, is an important historical landmark for comprehending the area's more extensive history. This fort, built in 1870, was part of a network of military outposts intended to subdue the Apache tribe during the chaotic period of westward expansion. Today, the fort provides guided tours, a museum, and access to the Apache Cultural Center, making it a valuable educational resource.

The Sedona Heritage Museum in Jordan Historical Park displays artifacts, images, and stories of Sedona's transformation from a tiny farming village to a modern tourist destination. The museum's exhibits cover various areas of Sedona life, such as the early cowboy days, the orchard business, and the production of Hollywood films in the area, giving visitors a thorough insight into local history.

Each trail in Sedona offers more than simply physical beauty; it also serves as a pathway through time. Hikers are traveling in the footsteps of individuals who made history in the heart of red rock country, whether it's the ancient rock art of the

Sinagua at V-Bar-V or pioneer pathways like the Munds Wagon Trail. For those willing to investigate, Sedona's trails provide a unique opportunity to connect with the past, with each hike serving as a journey of discovery and appreciation for the rich tapestry of human history woven into this remarkable terrain.

Outdoor Adventures in Sedona: Exciting Events for Nature Lovers

Sedona is more than simply a hiking haven; it's an outdoor enthusiast's dream come true. The bright environment of red rock formations, pine woods, and canyons offers endless activities that allow tourists to connect with Arizona's natural splendor. Sedona is a hotspot for outdoor activities, from bicycling rocky trails and scaling towering cliffs to kayaking peaceful canals. With its extensive calendar of hiking festivals, guided excursions, and outdoor events, Sedona has something for everyone, whether you're an adrenaline junkie or someone looking for a calm communion with nature.

Hiking and Trail Exploration

Sedona has nearly 300 miles of trails that cater to all experience levels, from easy treks to challenging ascents. For anyone seeking to experience Sedona's distinctive outdoor activity, these paths are a great place to begin:

Devil's Bridge trek: Known for its natural sandstone arch, this somewhat difficult trek provides breathtaking views and an exciting experience crossing the Bridge.

West Fork Trail: Perfect for a day trek, this trail meanders along Oak Creek and is shaded by trees, making it an excellent choice on hot days.

Bear Mountain Trail: This challenging but rewarding trek provides panoramic views of Sedona's most renowned formations.

Each path allows you to immerse yourself in Sedona's stunning vistas while learning about the area's unique geological heritage.

Mountain Bike Adventures

Sedona is a world-class mountain biking destination with trails winding through the red rock landscapes. Whether you're a beginner or an experienced rider, you'll find trails that test your abilities while rewarding you with breathtaking views.

Bell Rock Pathway: This walk is ideal for novices, with gentle hills and well-maintained trails.

Mescal Trail: Popular among expert riders, this trail features challenging terrain and exhilarating descents.

Hiline track: Renowned for its advanced technical challenges and panoramic views, this track is ideal for experienced riders looking for a thrill.

Local bike rental businesses and guided excursions make it simple to get started, even if you are new to the sport.

Rock climbing and canyoneering

Sedona's towering cliffs and deep canyons make it an ideal destination for rock climbing and canyoneering. Climbers are drawn to sites with climbs of varying difficulty, such as Cathedral Rock and The Mace. For those new to climbing, guided excursions provide the equipment and skills to safely enjoy the excitement of ascending Sedona's red rock walls.

Canyoneers will appreciate exploring slot gorges and rappelling down waterfalls in the nearby area. The Verde

Valley and Oak Creek Canyon are famous destinations for these thrilling activities.

Water Activities

Despite being in a desert location, Sedona has many water-related activities. Oak Creek runs through Sedona and is a refreshing refuge for cooling down on hot days.

Kayaking and paddleboarding: The Verde River offers a serene and picturesque setting for kayaking and paddleboarding. Paddlers can enjoy the lush scenery and plentiful wildlife.

Swimming and wading: Popular destinations such as Slide Rock State Park feature natural water slides and pools, making it a popular choice for families and anyone wishing to unwind by the water.

Oak Creek is also an excellent spot for fly fishing, with rainbow trout being the most typical catch. Local outfitters can provide equipment and assistance to ensure a good day on the water.

Camping and stargazing

Sedona's secluded setting and little light pollution make it ideal for stargazing. After a day of touring, camp at one of the authorized spots and enjoy the undisturbed night sky.

Popular campgrounds include Manzanita and Cave Springs Campground, which provide access to surrounding trails and waterways.

Stargazing Events: Sedona's classification as an International Dark Sky Community ensures spectacular vistas of the universe. Many local guides provide nighttime tours that mix hiking and telescope viewing.

Upcoming events for outdoor enthusiasts.

Sedona's outdoor culture extends beyond its trails and activities, with various events designed for hikers, adventurers, and environment lovers. Here's a look at upcoming gatherings and festivals that highlight Sedona's outdoor spirit:

The Sedona Mountain Bike Festival: held every spring, is a three-day celebration of all things mountain biking. Riders from all over the country visit Sedona to explore its legendary routes, attend clinics, and join group rides. The festival also features live music, food trucks, and gear demonstrations.

Hike Sedona Week: is an annual event with guided hikes, trail maintenance activities, and educational talks on Sedona's ecology and geology. It's an excellent opportunity for hikers to meet with local experts and explore paths they might not have found on their own.

Sedona Starlight Hike: A seasonal favorite, this guided twilight hike mixes stars and storytelling. Participants follow a leisurely walk while learning about constellations, Sedona's dark sky efforts, and the cultural significance of the stars.

Verde Valley Birding & environment Festival: Bird watchers and environment enthusiasts gather at this springtime festival that displays Sedona's abundant biodiversity. The activities include guided birding walks, environmental photography courses, and wildlife talks.

The Sedona Trail Run Series: is ideal for people who appreciate combining training and environmental discovery. The events range from 5K to half-marathon distances on circuits highlighting Sedona's most scenic vistas.

The Sedona Yoga Festival: provides lessons and programs in natural settings for people seeking a deeper spiritual connection with the outdoors. Events include outdoor yoga sessions, meditation treks, and holistic wellness seminars.

Slide Rock State Park Apple Festival: This family-friendly festival honors Sedona's agricultural legacy and the natural splendor of Slide Rock State Park. Visitors can ride hay, pick apples, and watch old-fashioned apple-pressing demonstrations.

Responsible for outdoor exploration.

As more people discover the delights of Sedona, it becomes more crucial to preserve its natural beauty. Visitors are asked to follow Leave No Trace practices, such as keeping on identified routes, removing all garbage, and preserving wildlife habitats. Many Sedona events contain conservation components, such as trail cleanups and sustainable tourism training.

Sedona's combination of outdoor activities and entertaining events distinguishes it as a top destination for explorers and nature lovers. Whether hiking a remote route, kayaking down a tranquil river, or attending one of the numerous outdoor events, Sedona provides an opportunity to connect with the natural world meaningfully. Sedona's ever-changing terrain and lively outdoor culture stimulate year-round exploration and appreciation.

Sedona Hike: A Photographer's Paradise.

Sedona, Arizona, is a photographer's dream, with its vibrant colors, textures, and light. Sedona, known for its unique red rock formations and bright vistas, is home to some of the world's most attractive natural beauty. Whether you're a seasoned photographer or a hobbyist with a keen eye, Sedona's various landscapes offer numerous opportunities to capture the ideal snap. This chapter will take you through the top photographic sites in Sedona and provide advice for shooting the perfect sunset, ensuring you leave with stunning photographs and wonderful memories.

Photographic Hotspots

Exploring Sedona is similar to wandering through a live gallery, with each turn providing a new opportunity to capture nature's artistry. Here are some of the best places where the views are not only spectacular but also quite photogenic:

Cathedral Rock

This magnificent sandstone formation is one of Sedona's most photographed attractions. With its commanding presence and remarkable symmetry, Cathedral Rock provides a dramatic backdrop for photographers. The neighboring Red Boulder Crossing reflects this enormous boulder perfectly in the waters of Oak Creek, which is especially beautiful at sunrise and dusk.

Bell Rock

Bell Rock, known for its distinctive bell shape, captivates tourists with its smooth, flowing lines and how it changes color in response to the sun. The trails around Bell Rock offer a variety of viewpoints and compositions, with juniper trees in the foreground providing a harsh contrast to the rock's flawless lines.

Airport Mesa

Airport Mesa offers panoramic views of Sedona. The overlook provides a 360-degree view of the surrounding environment, perfect for sunrise and sunset photography. The elevated position provides a unique view of the town and its renowned red rocks, notably Coffee Pot Rock.

Devil's Bridge

Devil's Bridge, Sedona's most significant natural sandstone arch, creates a spectacular picture for photographers. The trek to the Bridge is an adventure in and of itself, with a magnificent perspective that is best photographed early in the morning to avoid crowds and capture the soft, diffuse light.

Oak Creek Canyon

A trip down Oak Creek Canyon exposes a verdant riparian habitat that contrasts starkly with the red rock walls. Stop at Slide Rock State Park to shoot the smooth, water-worn boulders and tumbling water, or take in the towering canyon walls from one of the many roadside pullouts.

Tips for capturing the perfect sunset.

Sedona's sunsets are nothing short of breathtaking, painting the sky in shades of orange, pink, and red that reflect off the red rocks, producing a flaming glow. Here are some tips to help you capture these captivating moments:

Plan your spot.

Sunset photography begins well before the golden hour. Scout your area during the day, design your composition, and determine where the sun will set. Apps such as PhotoPills and The Photographer's Ephemeris can assist you in predicting the sun's location and light quality at various times of day.

Arrive early.

Arrive at your preferred location at least an hour before sunset to catch the entire Spectrum of colors. This allows you to set up without rushing and capture the changing light before and after the sun sets below the horizon.

Use the right equipment.

A tripod is necessary for steadiness, significantly when light levels decrease. Use a graduated neutral density filter to equalize the exposure between the bright sky and the dark countryside. A remote shutter release or your camera's timer function can also help prevent camera wobble.

Experiment With Settings

Begin with a tiny aperture (high f-number) to keep the foreground and background finely focused. Adjust the shutter speed based on the light, and don't be afraid to change the ISO settings if necessary. Bracket your exposures to capture all light levels, which you can mix for the final photo.

Capture the colors of Twilight.

Do not pack up your gear quite yet after the sun has set. The sky often brightens up with even more dramatic colors during the blue hour, which occurs shortly after sunset when the sky turns a deep blue and the first stars appear.

Pay attention to composition.

Use the rule of thirds to position the horizon and other essential components, such as rock formations. Look for leading lines or natural characteristics to help the viewer navigate the image. Foreground objects such as rocks, plants, or water can enhance the depth and intrigue of your sunset photographs.

Sedona's distinctive geological features and almost ethereal lighting make it a photographer's dream destination. Whether shooting expansive views, personal landscapes, or the sublime majesty of a Sedona sunset, the possibilities for spectacular photography are endless. Remember that the best photo is more than just the location; it's about capturing a moment in time, a feeling, and the pure joy of being in one of the most beautiful places on the planet. With these suggestions and locations in mind, you may make stunning images that capture the enchantment of Sedona.

Shopping In Sedona: A Treasure Trove of Unique Finds and Local Crafts.

Nestled amidst Arizona's spectacular red rocks, Sedona is more than just a retreat for nature lovers and spiritual searchers; it's also a thriving shopping destination for those looking for one-of-a-kind, locally-made things and memorable mementos. From fancy galleries to charming street-side stalls, shopping in Sedona is as much about the experience as it is about the products you purchase. In this guide, we'll look at the most significant shopping districts, highlight local handicrafts and souvenirs, and give recommendations for making your shopping trip in Sedona as rewarding as possible.

Best Shopping Districts in Sedona

Uptown Sedona: is the city's primary shopping district, teeming with activity and filled with businesses to suit every taste and price. Chic boutiques, fine art galleries, casual souvenir shops, and pleasant cafes are available here. The bustling environment is enhanced by breathtaking views of the neighboring red cliffs, making Uptown an ideal starting place for any shopping trip.

Tlaquepaque Arts & Shopping Village: inspired by a traditional Mexican village, is a must-see destination for anybody interested in arts and crafts. This picturesque arts hamlet features cobblestone roads, charming courtyards, and a variety of specialty stores and galleries displaying the work of local and international artists. Whether you're looking for beautiful art, handmade jewelry, or artisan furniture, Tlaquepaque provides a one-of-a-kind shopping experience that feels far from ordinary.

The Hozho District: on Gallery Row features luxury galleries and businesses focusing on Native American and modern art. This calm, sophisticated area of Sedona is excellent for people wishing to invest in quality artwork and sculpture. The galleries here frequently feature artist demos and gallery tours, which provide visitors with a more in-depth understanding of the creative process.

West Sedona: offers a more local shopping experience, with grocery stores, bakeries, and local diners interspersed with boutiques and booksellers. It's a terrific spot to get valuable and one-of-a-kind local goods without paying too much, like in more major shopping districts.

Local Handicrafts and Souvenirs

Sedona is known for its intense arts scene and spiritual significance, which are reflected in the local handicrafts for sale. Here are some must-haves:

Native American Crafts Sedona and the surrounding surroundings have a long history of Native American culture, which is frequently shown in local shops. Look for hand-woven Navajo rugs, Hopi kachinas, and beautiful Zuni jewelry. These pieces are not just gorgeous; they also carry the history and traditions of their creators.

Consider Sedona Red Rock Sand Art for a truly one-of-a-kind souvenir—beautifully layered sand masterpieces that replicate the natural striations of the area's iconic terrain. These art creations take numerous forms, ranging from simple bottles to elaborate landscapes and capture the essence of Sedona in a creative and earthy manner.

Given Sedona's image as a spiritual destination, it's no wonder that many businesses sell crystals, tarot decks, and essential oils. These make for thoughtful gifts or personal keepsakes that capture the city's mysterious spirit.

Sedona's artistic culture is growing, with many local artists deriving inspiration from the breathtaking natural beauty surrounding them. Pick up a painting, sculpture, or pottery to bring some of Sedona's artistic flair into your house.

Shopping Tips

Know When to Visit: Many shops in Sedona have seasonal hours, with extended hours throughout the tourist season from spring to fall. Plan your shopping expeditions early in the day to avoid the afternoon throng and have first access to the unusual things on show.

Attend Local Art Walks and Markets: Sedona organizes various art walks and local markets throughout the year, providing excellent opportunities to meet artists and purchase unique works at lower costs. These events are frequently accompanied by live music and food stalls, creating a festive shopping atmosphere.

Bargain Respectfully: While bargaining is permitted in some markets, especially with street sellers, it is critical to do so respectfully. Many products, particularly art and handicrafts, are priced to represent the effort and expertise put into them, so think about the piece's worth before negotiating.

Explore Off the Beaten Path While large shopping districts are convenient, more minor, off-the-beaten-path businesses can provide unique treasures and less congested shopping experiences. Take the time to explore outside the central locations; you might find the ideal item tucked away in a quiet nook of Sedona.

Shopping in Sedona is more than retail therapy; it investigates local culture, art, and spirit. Whether you're seeking great art to hang on your walls, a piece of jewelry to carry the energy of Sedona with you, or simply a tiny keepsake from your trip, Sedona's shops have a variety of treasures waiting to be discovered. Happy shopping!

Practical Travel Information for Sedona: Essentials for A Safe And Enjoyable Trip

With its breathtaking red rock panoramas and bustling art scene, Sedona attracts visitors worldwide. You must know the local health services, safety requirements, cultural norms, and communication infrastructure to maximize your vacation to this Arizona jewel. This thorough book includes the practical information you'll need for a pleasant and memorable stay in Sedona.

Health and Medical Services

Access to Healthcare Sedona is well-equipped to meet various medical needs, with institutions such as the Verde Valley Medical Center in adjacent Cottonwood, which provides extensive medical services, and the Sedona Medical Center, which offers urgent care and outpatient treatments. Pharmacy and wellness centers are also widely available across the city, providing everything from prescription services to holistic health treatments.

Hospital and Clinics

Verde Valley Medical Center: is a full-service hospital located around 20 miles from Sedona that provides emergency services, inpatient and outpatient treatment, advanced surgical procedures, and a heart center.

Sedona Medical Center: offers urgent care services, making it an easy choice for non-emergency situations, including minor injuries and illnesses.

Spectrum Healthcare: Besides primary care, Spectrum provides mental health treatments and is available to travelers who require non-urgent medical assistance.

Alternative Medicine Sedona is known for its spiritual and healing community. Acupuncture, massage, energy therapy, and naturopathy are among the treatments offered by numerous institutes. Sedona offers a wide range of alternative therapies.

Safety Tips

trekking Safety Sedona's trails are gorgeous, but they may be dangerous, particularly for individuals unfamiliar with desert trekking.

Stay Hydrated: The arid climate dehydrates you quickly. Carry plenty of water.

Wear Appropriate Gear: Durable footwear and sun protection (hats, sunscreen) are essential.

Stay on marked trails: Stay on marked trails to ensure your safety and the protection of the delicate desert habitat.

Check the weather: Flash floods and lightning are possible during the monsoon season (July to September).

Wildlife Precautions: While encounters with wildlife are uncommon, be wary of snakes, scorpions, and mountain lions.

Be alert: Be alert at dawn and dusk, when wildlife is most active.

Maintain a Safe Distance: If you encounter any wildlife, keep a safe distance and do not attempt to feed or touch them.

Personal Safety Sedona is generally a safe place. However, like with any trip destination, it is critical to follow standard safety procedures.

Secure Your Belongings: Keep valuables in hotel safes and avoid leaving goods visible in your car.

Stay Informed: Keep up to speed on local news, particularly weather conditions and area advisories.

Common Local Customs and Etiquette

Respect for Nature Sedona's community values its natural surroundings, which many hold sacred.

Leave No Trace: Always clean up after yourself and adhere to standards to reduce your impact on the natural world.

Cultural Sites: Many locations in and around Sedona hold cultural significance for Native American tribes. Please respect these places by not removing artifacts or defacing rock formations.

Tipping Etiquette: Tipping is traditional in Sedona and around the United States.

Restaurants charge 15-20% of the total, depending on the level of service.

Tour guides and activity instructors charge $5 to $10 per participant for group activities and 10-15% for individual excursions.

Interactions with Locals Sedonans are recognized for their warmth and relaxed demeanor.

Greeting: A simple "hello" or "good morning" is usual.

Ask Before Photographing: If you want to photograph locals or their property, ask for permission first.

Staying connected (WiFi and Communication)

Internet Access: Most hotels, cafes, and restaurants in Sedona provide free WiFi to their clients. For individuals needing more reliable connectivity, the Sedona Public Library offers free internet services, and some internet cafes charge a fee for computer use.

Mobile Connectivity: Sedona has decent coverage from major US mobile providers. However, isolated regions near canyons and national forest land may have poor service. If you intend to travel outside urban areas, check with your carrier regarding coverage options.

In the event of an emergency, phone 911. This number is suitable for fire, police, and medical situations.

Visiting Sedona allows you to experience its breathtaking scenery, interact with a distinct culture, and relax in its calm serenity. You may ensure a comfortable and enriching journey by making the necessary preparations for health, safety, and local customs and remaining connected. Keep this guide ready as you explore all that Sedona has to offer, making your visit memorable and hassle-free.

Conclusion: Maximizing Your Sedona Experience.

As you wind down your Sedona vacation, reflecting on the various activities offered in this colorful and mysterious city is essential. Sedona is more than just a tourist attraction; it's a journey through a breathtakingly beautiful and spiritually enlightening landscape. Every moment spent here, from the stunning red rock formations to the inviting community, has the potential to be transformative. Here are some last-minute travel suggestions, methods for maximizing your visit, and final thoughts to make your Sedona trip as gratifying and memorable as possible.

Last-Minute Travel Tips

Check weather: Check the Weather Sedona's weather can change dramatically with the seasons. Even day-to-night temperature changes can be significant, especially in the spring and fall. Check the local weather forecast before heading out each day so you can dress appropriately and plan your activities. This is especially crucial if you plan to walk, as unexpected weather changes might make trails difficult.

Pack effectively: Packaging effectively is essential given the variety of activities, including hiking, bicycling, gallery hopping, and gourmet dining. Include a mix of casual clothing for daytime adventures and better gear for evenings. Comfortable walking shoes, a hat, sunglasses, sunscreen, and a reusable water bottle are all essentials for staying hydrated.

Plan Your itinerary: While Sedona is relatively small, it's a good idea to plan your itinerary ahead of time, especially if you're visiting popular attractions like Cathedral Rock or Bell Rock. To avoid crowds, see in the early morning or late afternoon. If you're renting a car, have a dependable GPS or updated maps, as cell reception might be erratic in more distant regions.

Make Reservations: Sedona has become a popular destination, and restaurants, tours, and lodging can fill up quickly, especially during peak tourist seasons. Book everything in advance to minimize disappointment, from your hotel accommodation to guided excursions and fancy dinners. This is especially vital for hot-air balloon excursions, jeep trips, and fine dining establishments that offer views of the Red Rocks.

How to make the most of your visit

Engage with Local Culture: Sedona has a rich cultural past and contemporary art. Visit local museums, art shows, or the Tlaquepaque Arts & Shopping Village to see and buy work by local artisans. Engage with the artists and shop owners; their experiences will broaden your appreciation of the area and add a personal touch to the goods you carry home.

While Sedona's most famous monuments are well worth seeing, don't hesitate to wander off the well-trodden road. Lesser-known trails, such as the Doe Mountain Trail, provide beautiful views without the crowds. Similarly, visiting the neighboring wineries or taking a picturesque drive down Oak Creek Canyon might offer a fresh perspective on the area's natural splendor.

Take Time to Reflect One of Sedona's greatest assets is its ability to provide opportunities for introspection and regeneration. Take time to reflect on your experiences, whether through meditation at one of the vortex sites or simply watching the sunset from a quiet spot. Sedona is a place that fosters reflection and connection, so give yourself time to absorb its transforming spirit fully.

Final Thought

As your journey to Sedona comes to an end, take some time to reflect on your experiences. Sedona provides many opportunities to reconnect with nature and nourish your spirit, whether it's the thrill of trekking the red rocks, the tranquility of a sunrise yoga practice, or the delight of discovering an unexpected art gallery. The memories you create here will last long after you return home.

Each visit to Sedona is as unique as the breathtaking scenery. Whether you return year after year or consider this a once-in-a-lifetime experience, the charm of Sedona will leave an indelible impact on your heart. Remember that Sedona is more than simply a destination; it is an experience that stays long after you leave its brilliant cliffs and tranquil landscapes.

Appendix

Useful Apps

AllTrails - Ideal for finding the best hiking trails in and around Sedona, complete with user reviews and filter options based on difficulty, length, and scenic views.

Sedona Trail Finder - Offers detailed maps and navigation for Sedona's extensive trail network, helping you to safely explore the wilderness.

OpenTable - Useful for making reservations at Sedona's popular restaurants, ensuring you secure a spot, especially during peak seasons.

Star Walk - Perfect for stargazing in Sedona, this app helps you identify constellations, planets, and stars in the clear Sedona night sky.

Weather Underground - Provides reliable, up-to-date weather forecasts to help plan your outdoor activities in Sedona.

Travel Checklist

- Comfortable hiking boots/shoes
- Weather-appropriate clothing (layers recommended)

- Wide-brimmed hat, sunglasses, and sunscreen
- Reusable water bottle
- Daypack for hikes and excursions
- Camera or smartphone with extra batteries/charger
- Personal identification and insurance information
- Copies of travel reservations (digital and physical)
- First aid kit
- Snacks for trail hikes

Emergency Contacts

Sedona Police Department: +1 928-282-3100

Verde Valley Medical Center (Cottonwood): +1 928-634-2251

Sedona Fire Department: +1 928-282-6800

Poison Control: +1 800-222-1222

Roadside Assistance: Check with your car rental provider or insurance for specific numbers.

Frequently Asked Questions

What is the best time of year to visit Sedona?

- Spring (March to May) and fall (September to November) offer mild weather, making these seasons ideal for hiking and outdoor activities.

Are the hiking trails in Sedona suitable for beginners?

- Yes, Sedona has a variety of trails ranging from easy walks to more challenging hikes. Bell Rock Pathway and Sedona View Trail are great for beginners.

What are the must-see attractions in Sedona?

- The must-see attractions include Cathedral Rock, Bell Rock, Chapel of the Holy Cross, and the Sedona Arts Center.

Is it necessary to rent a car in Sedona?

- While some areas are walkable, a car rental is highly recommended for convenience and to explore more distant attractions and trailheads.

Can I visit the Grand Canyon from Sedona for a day trip?

- Yes, the Grand Canyon's South Rim is about a 2-hour drive from Sedona, making it feasible as a day trip.

Suggested Travel Itineraries

3-Day Itinerary

Day 1: Explore Uptown Sedona and Tlaquepaque Arts & Shopping Village. Dine at a local restaurant with views of the red rocks.

Day 2: Spend the day hiking. Start with Cathedral Rock in the morning and Bell Rock in the afternoon. Enjoy an evening stargazing tour.

Day 3: Visit the Chapel of the Holy Cross and then drive to Oak Creek Canyon for a picnic and relaxation by the water.

5-Day Itinerary

Day 1-3: Follow the 3-day itinerary.

Day 4: Take a jeep tour of the red rocks, visit Sedona Heritage Museum, and relax with a spa treatment.

Day 5: Drive to Jerome, an historic copper mining town nearby, and explore its art galleries and museums.

7-Day Itinerary

Day 1-5: Follow the 5-day itinerary.

Day 6: Visit the Verde Valley Wine Trail and enjoy tastings at local vineyards.

Day 7: Take a day trip to the Grand Canyon or explore more remote trails and sights in the Sedona area.

Made in the USA
Monee, IL
22 March 2025